OBSERVATIONS

Also by Henry Kissinger

A WORLD RESTORED: CASTLEREAGH, METTERNICH AND THE
RESTORATION OF PEACE 1812–1822

NUCLEAR WEAPONS AND FOREIGN POLICY

THE NECESSITY FOR CHOICE: PROSPECTS OF AMERICAN
FOREIGN POLICY

THE TROUBLED PARTNERSHIP: A RE-APPRAISAL OF THE
ATLANTIC ALLIANCE

AMERICAN FOREIGN POLICY

WHITE HOUSE YEARS

FOR THE RECORD: SELECTED STATEMENTS 1977–1980

YEARS OF UPHEAVAL

as editor: PROBLEMS OF NATIONAL STRATEGY:
A BOOK OF READINGS

OBSERVATIONS

Selected Speeches and Essays
1982–1984

Henry Kissinger

Little, Brown and Company • Boston • Toronto

FIRST EDITION

"After Lebanon: A Conversation," reprinted with permission from *The Economist,* London, November 13, 1982.

LIBRARY OF CONGRESS CATALOGING IN PUBLICATION DATA

Kissinger, Henry A., 1923-
   Observation : selected speeches and essays, 1982-1984.

   Includes index.
   1. United States—Foreign relations—1981-
—Addresses, essays, lectures.   I. Title.
E838.5.K582 1985   327.73   85-199
ISBN 0-316-49664-2

VB

*Published simultaneously in Canada
by Little, Brown & Company (Canada) Limited*

PRINTED IN THE UNITED STATES OF AMERICA

To
Agnes McKinley Maginnes

CONTENTS

Foreword   ix

Reflections on a Partnership: British and American   1
   Attitudes to Postwar Foreign Policy
     May 1982

Strategy, Trade, and the Atlantic Alliance   27
     May 1982

From Lebanon to the West Bank to the Gulf   49
     June 1982

American Global Concerns and Africa   57
     September 1982

Challenges to the West in the 1980s   77
     September 1982

After Lebanon: A Conversation   91
     November 1982

How to Deal with Moscow   111
     November 1982

Saving the World Economy   125
     January 1983

Mr. Shultz Goes to China: What Should Come   139
   Out of This Trip
     January 1983

A New Approach to Arms Control   151
     March 1983

Issues before the Atlantic Alliance   165
     January 1984

Statement of the Chairman of the President's National   189
  Bipartisan Commission on Central America to the Senate
  Foreign Relations Committee
    February 1984

A Plan to Reshape NATO   201
    March 1984

International Economics and World Order   219
    September 1984

Index   237

FOREWORD

THE PROFESSOR turned policymaker faces a special problem when he returns to the role of commentator. He knows that policymakers are overwhelmed with advice; their dominant experience is their inability to give adequate attention to all the problems that face them at any one moment. At the same time, experience has taught the new outsider that the problems of which the policymaker is aware are the most urgent, not necessarily the most important. Once having been involved in policymaking, the returned academic should have learned that no outsider is in a position to offer day-to-day advice. He can never acquire enough of the details, mastery of which is the prerequisite for the sense of nuance that spells the difference between shaping events or being dominated by them. The proper role for the outsider is to raise the middle and long-term issues that the press of business keeps from the policymaker. In short, it is rarely possible to contribute to tactics and only occasionally to foreign policy directions and purposes.

The reader will have to judge to what extent I have been able to observe these maxims in my essays and interviews in recent years. They were put forward during a period that should have made for dispassion on my part. The foreign policy of America was the responsibility of the party that had given me the opportunity to serve my country. But its leaders chose a rhetoric explicitly hostile to the premises of its Republican predecessors. Despite this, I have agreed with most of the policies of the Reagan Administration even when I was less than ecstatic about the manner of their presentation and justification. All this encouraged a somewhat detached, if not philosophical, frame of mind. As time went on the Administration came to grips with the first rule of statesmanship: to master the scope available for creative action. To go beyond those limits is to court disaster; not to exploit it risks sterility.

I believe that the Administration, partly by design, partly by a combination of historical circumstances, has an opportunity to make a number of historical breakthroughs in East-West relations, in dealing with our allies, and in the encouragement of developing nations. These speeches and articles produced for special occasions can only sketch some of the roads open to us. They can raise some questions, which, if they are meritorious, others must answer in the fullness of time.

I would like to thank my editor, Genevieve Young, for her encouragement; Betsy Pitha, for her copyediting skills; and Rosemary N. Niehuss of my staff for her indispensable help in getting this volume ready for publication.

I have dedicated this book to my mother-in-law, Agnes McKinley Maginnes, whose friendship and kindness have meant a great deal to me.

February 1985   Henry Kissinger

REFLECTIONS ON A PARTNERSHIP

British and American Attitudes to Postwar Foreign Policy

Address commemorating the Bicentenary of the Office of Foreign Secretary, delivered at the Royal Institute of International Affairs, London, May 10, 1982

INTRODUCTION

MICHAEL HOWARD has confirmed what I had suspected: that the United States deserves some of the credit for Britain's decision to create a Foreign Office in the first place. The Foreign Office was founded only a few months after the battle of Yorktown. The "politicians" of the time having just mislaid America, the need was evidently felt for some more professional machinery to run Britain's newly expanded sphere of "foreign" affairs.

Since then, Britain and America have never ceased to play important roles in each other's history. On the whole it has been a productive and creative relationship, perhaps one of the most durable in the history of nations. In the last 200 years, we have approached each other sometimes warily, and dealt with foreign affairs often from different perspectives. Still, on balance the relationship has been of considerable benefit to world peace. This has been true particularly of the period since the Second World War.

All accounts of the Anglo-American alliance during the Second World War and in the early postwar period draw attention to the significant differences in philosophy between Franklin Roosevelt and Winston Churchill, reflecting our different national histories. America, which had never experienced a foreign threat to its survival, considered wars an historical aberration caused by evil men or institutions; we were preoccupied with victory defined as the unconditional surrender of the Axis. Britain had seen aggression take too many forms to risk so personal a view of history; she had her eyes on the postwar world and sought to gear wartime strategy toward forestalling Soviet domination of Central Europe. Many American leaders condemned Churchill as needlessly obsessed with power politics, too rigidly anti-Soviet, too colonialist in his attitude to what is now called the Third World, and too little interested in building the fundamentally new international order toward which American idealism has always tended. The British undoubtedly saw the Americans as naive, moralistic, and evading responsibility for helping secure the global equilibrium. The dispute was resolved according to American preferences — in my view, to the detriment of postwar security.

Fortunately, Britain had a decisive influence over America's rapid awakening to maturity in the years following. In the 1940s and 1950s our two countries responded together to the geopolitical challenge of the Soviet Union and took the lead in creating the structures of Western cooperation for the postwar era which brought a generation of security and prosperity.

In the process a rather ironic reversal of positions took place. Today it is the United States that is accused of being obsessesd with the balance of power, and it is our European allies who are charged by us with moralistic escapism.

I believe that the extraordinary partnership among the democracies will overcome the occasional squabbles that form the headlines of the day and, even more important, meet the objective new challenges that our countries face.

PHILOSOPHIES OF FOREIGN POLICY

The disputes between Britain and America during the Second World War and after were, of course, not an accident. British policy drew upon two centuries of experience with the European balance of power, America on two centuries of rejecting it.

Where America had always imagined itself isolated from world affairs, Britain for centuries was keenly alert to the potential danger that any country's domination of the European continent — whatever its domestic structure or method of dominance — placed British survival at risk. Where Americans have tended to believe that wars were caused by the moral failure of leaders, the British view is that aggression has thrived on opportunity as much as on moral propensity, and must be restrained by some kind of balance of power. Where Americans treated diplomacy as episodic — a series of isolated problems to be solved on their merits — the British have always understood it as an organic historical process requiring constant manipulation to keep it moving in the right direction.

Britain has rarely proclaimed moral absolutes or rested her faith in the ultimate efficacy of technology, despite her achievements in this field. Philosophically, she remains Hobbesian: she expects the worst and is rarely disappointed. In moral matters Britain has traditionally practiced a convenient form of ethical egoism, believing that what was good for Britain was best for the rest. This requires a certain historical self-confidence, not to say nerve, to carry it off. But she has always practiced it with an innate moderation and civilized humaneness such that her presumption was frequently justified. In the nineteenth century, British policy was a — perhaps *the* — principal factor in a European system that kept the peace for ninety-nine years without a major war.

American foreign policy is the product of a very different tradition. The founding fathers, to be sure, were sophisticated men who understood the European balance of power and skillfully manipulated it to win independence. But for a century and more after that, America, comfortably protected by two oceans — which in turn were secured by the Royal Navy — developed the idiosyncratic notion that a fortunate accident was a natural state of affairs, that our involvement in world politics was purely a matter of choice. Where George Canning viewed the Monroe Doctrine in terms of the world equilibrium, "call[ing] the New World into existence to redress the balance of the Old," Americans imagined the entire Western hemisphere a special case, safely insulated from the rest of the world. We had created a nation consciously dedicated to "self-evident" truths, and it was taken for granted in most American public discourse that our participation (or non-participation) in the world could be guided exclusively by moral precepts. That geography gave us this luxury was only evidence of God's blessing upon us; we owed Him that quid pro quo. The competitive, sometimes cynical, and always relativistic style of European power politics was viewed in America as an unsavory example of what to avoid and as further evidence of our moral superiority.

In American discussion of foreign policy, even through much of the twentieth century, the phrase "balance of power" was hardly ever written or spoken without a pejorative adjective in front of it — the "outmoded" balance of power, the "discredited" balance of power. When Woodrow Wilson took America into the First World War, it was in the expectation that under American influence the postwar settlement would be governed by a "new and more wholesome diplomacy," transcending the wheeling and dealing, secrecy, and undemocratic practices that were thought to have produced the Great War. Franklin Roosevelt, on his return from the Crimean Conference in 1945, told the Congress on March 1 of his hope that the postwar era would "spell the end of the system of unilateral action, the exclusive alliances, the spheres of influence, the balances of power, and all the other expedients that have been tried for centuries — and have always failed." Both Wilson and Roosevelt put their faith in a universal organization of collective security in which the peace-loving nations would combine to deter, or combat, the aggressors. It was assumed that all nations would come to the same conclusions regarding what constituted aggression and be equally willing to resist it, no matter where it occurred, regardless of how far from their borders, irrespective of the national interest involved.

In the American view, nations were either inherently peaceful or inherently warlike. Hence, after World War II the "peace-loving" United States, Britain, and USSR had together to police the world against Germany and Japan even though the former enemies had been rendered impotent by unconditional surrender. If there were doubts about the peace-loving virtue of our wartime allies, they seemed to many American leaders to apply as much to Britain as to the USSR: Roosevelt toyed with the idea of nonalignment between a balance-of-power-oriented, colonialist Britain and an ideologically obstreperous Soviet Union. Even Truman took care not to meet with Churchill in advance of the Potsdam Conference; he did not want to appear to be "lining up" with Britain against the USSR. The secret dream of American leaders, if great-power conflict proved unavoidable, was to arrogate to themselves the role to which the nonaligned later aspired: that of moral arbiter, hurling condescending judgments down at all those engaged in the dirty game of international diplomacy.

As late as 1949, the Department of State submitted to the Senate Foreign Relations Committee a memorandum that strove mightily to distinguish the new North Atlantic Treaty from traditional military alliances and above all from any relationship to the very balance of power it was supposed to establish. The treaty, the memorandum said,

> is directed against no one; it is directed solely against aggression. It seeks not to influence any shifting "balance of power" but to strengthen the "balance of principle."*

American attitudes until the last ten years have embodied a faith that historical experience can be transcended, that problems can be solved permanently, that harmony can be the natural state of mankind. Thus our diplomacy has often stressed the concepts of international law, with its procedures of arbitration and peaceful settlement, as if all political disputes were legal issues, on the premise that reasonable men and women could always find agreement on some equitable basis. There is also a perennial American assumption that economic well-being automatically ensures political stability, a belief which has animated American policies from Herbert Hoover's relief efforts after World War I to the Marshall Plan to the recent Caribbean initiative — never mind that, in many parts of the world, the time frames for economic progress and the achievement of political stability may be seriously out of phase. In our participation in the two world wars of this century, and afterward, our bursts of energy were coupled with the conviction that our exertions had a terminal date, after which the natural harmony among nations would be either restored or instituted.

Disillusionment was inevitable. America fluctuated between moral crusading and frustrated isolationism, between overextension

* U.S. Senate, Committee on Foreign Relations, *Hearings on the North Atlantic Treaty*, 81st Congress, 1st session (1949), part 1, Appendix, p. 337.

and escapism, between extremes of intransigence and conciliation. But history was kind to us. For a long time it spared us from the need to face up to fundamental choices. Not being called upon to help preserve the equilibrium — a service rendered gratis by Great Britain — we could avoid the responsibility of permanent involvement in world politics, of unending exertion with no final answers or ultimate resolution.   .

Even when the United States finally entered the world stage of permanent peacetime diplomacy after 1945, it did so under conditions that seemed to confirm our historical expectations. For several decades we had the overwhelming resources to give effect to our prescriptions, and thus conducted foreign policy by analogy with the great formative experiences of the 1930s and 1940s: the New Deal translated into the Marshall Plan; resistance to Nazi aggression translated into the Korean "police action" and the policy of "containment." We tended to attribute our dominance in the Western Alliance to the virtue of our motives rather than to the preponderance of our power. In fact, the United States enjoyed nearly half the world's Gross National Product and an atomic monopoly; our NATO allies, given their dependence, conducted themselves less as sovereign nations than as lobbyists in Washington decision-making.

It was therefore a rude awakening when in the 1960s and 1970s the United States became conscious of the limits of even *its* resources. Now with a little over a fifth of the world's GNP, America was powerful but no longer dominant. Vietnam was the trauma and the catharsis, but the recognition was bound to come in any event. Starting in the 1970s, for the first time, the United States has had to conduct a foreign policy in the sense with which Europeans have always been familiar: as one country among many, unable either to dominate the world or escape from it, with the necessity of accommodation, maneuver, a sensitivity to marginal shifts in the balance of power, an awareness of continuity and of the interconnections between events.

Our perennial domestic debates reflect the pain, and incompleteness, of that adjustment. The American Right still yearns for ideological victory without geopolitical effort; the American Left still dreams of reforming the world through the exercise of goodwill unsullied by power. We are edging toward a synthesis, but it will be a slow, painful, perhaps bitter process.

THE NATURE OF THE SPECIAL RELATIONSHIP

That two countries with such divergent traditions could form a durable partnership is remarkable in itself. The period of the close Anglo-American "special relationship," the object of such nostalgia today, were also times of occasional mutual exasperation.

For quite a while we stressed different aspects of our histories; in more senses than one, we lived in different time zones. It was only some while after the settlement of the *Alabama* affair just over a century ago that American and British interests began to run parallel. The need for intimacy seemed to be greater in Britain, and Britain began to avoid alliances that could entangle her against the United States — including a tantalizing offer from Germany around the turn of the century. American memories were longer; the First World War was a temporary exertion, after which we withdrew into isolationism; during the 1920s the US Navy Department still maintained a "Red Plan" to deal with the contingency of conflict with the British fleet.

It was not until the war with Hitler that the gap closed permanently. In the immediate postwar period we were held together by strategic circumstances which imposed the same necessities, whatever the different philosophical premises. American resources and organization and technological genius, and British experience and understanding of the European balance of power, were both needed to resist the sudden threat from the Soviet Union. The Marshall Plan and North Atlantic Treaty, while formally American initiatives, were inconceivable without British advice and British efforts to organize a rapid and effective European response. Ernest Bevin was the indispensable architect of the European response as well as the staunch helmsman of Britain's journey from power to influence.

Even then, Anglo-American difficulties persisted occasionally. The anguished disagreements over immigration into Palestine; the misunderstandings over atomic cooperation; competition over Iranian oil; the abrupt, unilateral ending of Lend-Lease; and the race to demobilize were only some of the items in a stream of irritants. More serious policy differences were to follow in the 1950s, causing Anthony Eden to reflect on the "tough reality of Anglo-American relations." Even when the politics were parallel, the personalities were often divergent. Eden and Dean Acheson were friends as well as colleagues; the same could not be said for Eden and John Foster Dulles. Misunderstandings and conflicts of interest continued through European integration, the rearmament of Germany, and Indochina, right up to the tragic climax of Suez — to which I will return in a few moments.

That these irritations never shook the underlying unity was due to statesmanship on both sides. One factor was a brilliant British adjustment to new circumstances. To the outside world it may have seemed that Britain clung far too long to the illusion of Empire; in her relations with Washington, she proved that an old country was beyond self-deception on fundamentals. Bevin, the unlikely originator of this revolution in British diplomacy, shrewdly calculated that Britain was not powerful enough to influence American policy by conventional methods of pressure or balancing of risks. But by discreet advice, the wisdom of experience, and the presupposition of common aims, she could make herself indispensable, so that American leaders no longer thought of consultations with London as a special favor but as an inherent component of our own decision-making. The wartime habit of intimate, informal collaboration thus became a permanent practice, obviously because it was valuable to both sides.

The ease and informality of the Anglo-American partnership has been a source of wonder — and no little resentment — to third countries. Our postwar diplomatic history is littered with Anglo-American "arrangements" and "understandings," sometimes on crucial issues, never put into formal documents. The stationing of B-29 atomic bombers in Britain in 1948 was agreed between political and service leaders but not committed to writing. Less happily, only general principles were recorded when Churchill and Roosevelt agreed in

1942 to cooperate in producing the atomic bomb. After Roosevelt died, Clement Attlee reflected with admirable restraint: "We were allies and friends. It didn't seem necessary to tie everything up." *

The British were so matter-of-factly helpful that they became a participant in internal American deliberations, to a degree probably never before practiced between sovereign nations. In my period in office, the British played a seminal part in certain American bilateral negotiations with the Soviet Union — indeed, they helped draft the key document. In my White House incarnation then, as I described in my memoirs, I kept the British Foreign Office better informed and more closely engaged than I did the American State Department — a practice which, with all affection for things British, I would not recommend be made permanent. But it was symptomatic.

For a brief moment in the early 1970s, Britain seemed to decide to put an end to the special relationship in order to prove itself a "good European" in the year that it entered the European Community. The attempt was short-lived. By 1976, James Callaghan and Anthony Crosland had restored the traditional close relationship — without resurrecting the label — and it was enormously valuable, indeed indispensable, in the Southern Africa negotiations that began in that year. In my negotiations over Rhodesia I worked from a British draft with British spelling even when I did not fully grasp the distinction between a working paper and a Cabinet-approved document. The practice of collaboration thrives to our day, with occasional ups and downs, but even in the recent Falkland crisis, an inevitable return to the main theme of the relationship.

Clearly, British membership in Europe has added a new dimension. But the solution, in my view, is not to sacrifice the special intimacy of the Anglo-American connection on the altar of the European idea, but rather to replicate it on a wider plane of America's relations with *all* its European allies, whether bilaterally or with a politically cohesive European Community. That is for Europe to decide. The special frankness and trust that may have been originally resorted to as compensation for a disparity of power may now be even more es-

* Clement Attlee and Francis Williams, *Twilight of Empire* (New York: A. S. Barnes & Co., 1962), p. 108.

sential in the partnership of equals that must characterize the future
relations between America and Europe.

BRITAIN, AMERICA, AND EUROPE

In fact, Europe has been a traumatic issue for both Britain and the
United States.

Americans often forget that Britain, too, has been a reluctant
internationalist, at least as far as Europe was concerned. Tradition
pulled Britain across distant oceans. The glory of foreign policy was
identified with Empire and Commonwealth, its problems and perils
with the continent of Europe. It was Czechoslovakia — in the heart
of Europe — which Chamberlain described as a small, faraway country of which Britons knew little, after a century and a half of fighting
on the borders of India.

In Britain, reluctance to enter Europe was always bipartisan,
and somewhat mystical. Eden once said that Britain knew "in her
bones" that she could not join it; and Hugh Gaitskell spoke of the impossibility of throwing off a thousand years of history. But there were
more substantial reasons: worries about sovereignty, which on the
Left were combined with concern for the unfettered development of
socialist planning; an instinctive disinclination to deal with continen-
tals on an equal footing; trade ties with the Commonwealth; and the
special relationship. Even Churchill, despite his intimations of the future, remained as ambivalent in government as he had been prescient
in opposition when he had called as early as 1947 for a United States
of Europe. In office, he never quite found the balance among his three
concentric circles — the Commonwealth, Europe, and the English-
speaking peoples.

Only after Suez did the risks of isolation become obvious, as well
as the opportunity that the emerging Europe offered for exercising in
a different but equally effective form Britain's traditional role of
guardian of continental equilibrium. If the economic benefits were
ambiguous, the political necessities were not: only as one of the lead-

ers of Europe could Britain continue to play a major role on the world scene.

By entering the European Community, Britain did not abandon her instinct for equilibrium. But for the first time in peacetime she threw herself into the scales. As I have already noted, she did so with the fervor of a frustrated convert who had been kept waiting for a decade at the doors of destiny.

If Britain has had a difficult adjustment to make in its relationship to Europe, so has the United States.

After the war, American leaders applied a heavy dose of our usual missionary zeal and the full rigor of our "problem-solving" energy to the task of promoting European integration. Federalism, of course, was a hallowed American principle. Shortly after the Philadelphia Convention, Benjamin Franklin was urging on the French the attractions of a federal Europe. A similar evangelism, in a more practical form, shone through the Marshall Plan. Even Acheson, not usually seen as a moralist, was carried away by the European idea; he recalled listening to Robert Schuman outlining his plan for a European Coal and Steel Community. "As he talked, we caught his enthusiasm and the breadth of his thought," Acheson wrote, "the rebirth of Europe, which, as an entity, had been in eclipse since the Reformation." *

Despite the idealism of our commitment, tensions between America and a unified Europe were inherent in the logic of what we were so enthusiastically endorsing. We had grown accustomed to the devastated, temporarily impotent Europe of the postwar period; we forgot the Europe that had launched the industrial revolution, that had invented the concept of national sovereignty, and that had operated a complex balance of power for three centuries. A Europe reasserting its personality was bound to seek to redress the balance of influence with the United States; Charles de Gaulle in this respect differed largely in method from Jean Monnet, who never disguised his hopes for a more powerful and effective European voice.

Thus, later American disillusionments were inherent in our

* Dean Acheson, *Sketches from Life* (New York: Harper & Bros., 1961), pp. 36–37.

goals. It was naive for Americans to take for granted that a federal
Europe would be more like us, that a united Europe would automati-
cally help carry our burdens, and that it would continue to follow
American global prescriptions as it had in the early postwar years of
European recovery — and dependency. That cannot be so.

Yet even if some of our more unhistorical expectations were
disappointed, our original judgment was correct: European unity,
strength, and self-confidence are essential for the future of the West.
It is beyond the psychological resources of the United States — not
only the physical — to be the sole or even the principal center of initiative and responsibility in the non-Communist world. (This is one
reason why I always favored the independent British and French nuclear deterrents.) American support for European unification was
therefore an expression of self-interest even if it paraded under the
banner of altruism; it was to our advantage even if we paid occasionally in the coin of clashing perspectives — provided we found a way
toward creative unity on fundamentals.

BRITAIN, EUROPE, THE UNITED STATES, AND THE SOVIET UNION

The central foreign policy problem that Britain, America, and Europe
have had to confront together since 1945 is, of course, the Soviet
Union. And the need for creative unity among us as we do so has not
ended.

One thing that is clear from the historical record is that neither
side of the Atlantic has had a monopoly of special insight into this
problem. As soon as the war had ended, both Britain and America fell
over each other in the rush to demobilize. All American troops were
due to leave Europe by 1947. After a visit to Moscow in May 1945,
Harry Hopkins told President Truman that he saw no major sources
of conflict between America and Russia on the horizon.*

_____

* Attlee and Williams, *Twilight of Empire*, p. 161.

After Churchill left office, British policy for a brief period ironically fell prey to some of the same illusions that had bedeviled American leaders. The Labour government at first hoped that "Left could speak unto Left." The brief moment of nostalgia reflected the hope that Britain would stand neither for the unbridled capitalism of the United States nor for Soviet Communism. A resolution calling for the "progressive unity" between the British Labour and Communist parties was only narrowly defeated. There is not much doubt, in fact, that once the United States was committed after the Greek-Turkish aid program in 1947, some in Britain were tempted — as Roosevelt and Truman were a few years earlier — by the idea of enhancing British influence by remaining aloof not just from Europe but from the emerging superpower confrontation, adding to Britain's traditional role as manipulator of the balance in Europe that of intermediary between East and West. This attitude has reappeared in some circles in Europe today.

No amount of revisionist distortion can change the fact that it was the Kremlin which turned Anglo-American hopes into mirages. There is today in some circles a curious assumption of diabolic Soviet cleverness and foresight. Yet in those years, Stalin's conduct of relations with his former allies made him the chief architect of NATO. A few more fleeting smiles on the wooden features of Mr. Molotov, and a modicum of self-restraint and diplomatic delicacy, would have done much to prise apart the young and still brittle Atlantic cooperation; and all the boys might have been home, as planned, by 1947.

The Soviets did not manage this degree of subtlety. Instead, Moscow went out of its way to estrange and alienate, where it could have softened through a little courtship, however heavy-handed. The Russians declined Britain's invitation to send a Soviet contingent to a victory parade, and Stalin sidestepped an offer from Attlee to renew the wartime alliance. Every door that Ernest Bevin, mindful of the influential left wing of his party, was careful to keep open was resoundingly slammed and loudly bolted. As was soon to be shown in the persecution of social democrats in Eastern Europe, the Soviet Union countenanced only one form of "socialism" and fought other, democratic versions even more bitterly than capitalists. The outright Soviet rejection of the Marshall Plan was an egregious blunder; a mild expression of interest, however disingenuous, could have caused untold disruption and delay in the Western camp. Acceptance would have changed the face of postwar politics.

It was one of those moments when America's activism and idealism brought out the best in her. The forties were years of imaginative men and bold measures on both sides of the Atlantic: the Marshall Plan, the Truman Doctrine, the Berlin airlift, the Brussels treaty, and finally NATO, were inspired and creative initiatives. And in the years following, the United States and its allies stood fast against Soviet pressures and blackmail in crises over Korea, Berlin, and missiles in Cuba.

But we in America had only begun to scratch the surface of the long-term problem of US–Soviet relations in the nuclear age, which would soon produce more ambiguous challenges. The problem was, at bottom, conceptual. Americans were uncomfortable with the notion of a cold war. They tended to treat war and peace as two distinct phases of policy. Total victory was the only legitimate goal for war; conciliation the appropriate method for peace. In this sense the postwar period fulfilled neither of America's conceptual expectations. If in wartime we lacked a sense of political strategy, in peacetime we had difficulty forming an understanding of the permanent relation between power and diplomacy. The policy of containment, and its variant called "negotiation from strength," was based on the experience with the anti-Hitler coalition. It focused on the buildup of military strength toward some hypothetical day of greater parity; it aimed at eventual negotiation of some kind with the Soviet Union but offered no clue as to either its timing or its content, nor even a clear definition of the nature of the relevant military strength. George Kennan's famous "X" article in *Foreign Affairs* in 1947 looked vaguely to the eventual "mellowing" of the Soviet system; Dean Acheson, in Senate hearings in 1951, spoke of building "situations of strength" which, somewhere down the road, would induce the Kremlin "to recognize the facts." But how precisely this negotiation would emerge or to what end it would be conducted was left vague.

The flaw in containment was not only, as the cliché has it today, that it was overly preoccupied with military counterforce but that it misunderstood that the West in the immediate postwar period was precisely at the apex of its relative strength. Containment thus deferred the moment for a diplomatic encounter with the Soviet Union to a later time by which Soviet power could only have grown. In 1945 the United States had an atomic monopoly and the Soviet Union was devastated by 20 million casualties. Our policy paradoxically gave the Kremlin time to consolidate its conquests and to redress the nuclear imbalance. The West's military and diplomatic position relative to the USSR was never more favorable than at the very *beginning* of the containment policy in the late forties. *That* was the time to attempt a serious discussion on the future of Europe and a peaceful world.

As so often, Winston Churchill understood it best. In a much-neglected speech at Llandudno on October 9, 1948, out of office, he said:

> The question is asked: What will happen when they get the atomic bomb themselves and have accumulated a large store? You can judge yourselves what will happen then by what is happening now. If these things are done in the green wood, what will be done in the dry? If they can continue month after month disturbing and tormenting the world, trusting to our Christian and altruistic inhibitions against using this strange new power against them, what will they do when they themselves have huge quantities of atomic bombs? . . . No one in his senses can believe that we have a limitless period of time before us. We ought to bring matters to a head and make a final settlement. We ought not to go jogging along improvident, incompetent, waiting for something to turn up, by which I mean waiting for something bad for us to turn up. The Western Nations will be far more likely to reach a lasting settlement, without bloodshed, if they formulate their just demands while they have the atomic power and before the Russian Communists have got it too.

So the postwar world came into being. A precarious peace was maintained, based on a nuclear equilibrium, with occasional negotiations to ease tensions temporarily, but ultimately dependent on a balance of terror. The problem of maintaining security took on an unprecedented new dimension. Technology was soon to make the United States directly vulnerable to attack; the Atlantic Alliance increasingly based its defense strategy on reliance on weapons of mass destruction that posed risks more and more difficult to reconcile with the objectives being defended.

In the nuclear age, peace became a moral imperative. And it imposed a new dilemma: the desire for peace is the mark of all civilized men and women. Yet the democracies' desire for peace, if divorced from a commitment to defend freedom, could turn into a weapon of blackmail in the hands of the most ruthless; if the desire to avoid nuclear war turns into undifferentiated hysteria, nuclear blackmail may well be encouraged. The problem of the relationship of power to peace, the balance between ends and means, has been evaded for a generation by an abdication to technology. But history tolerates no evasions. To develop a strategy that relates ends to means, to build military forces that avoid the choice between Armageddon and surrender, is a preeminent moral as well as political problem for our period. Of at least equal importance is to develop an Allied consensus behind proposals of arms control based on analysis, not panic, and freed of either the quest for confrontation or the tendency toward abdication.

THIRD WORLD PERSPECTIVES: WHAT IS THE LIMIT OF INTER-ALLIED CONFLICT?

In a period of nuclear stalemate, ironically, conflict became more likely at the level of local, nonnuclear crisis. In an age of decolonization, many of these clashes were bound to occur in the Third World. This was another area in which, in the immediate postward period, American and European attitudes diverged sharply.

Americans from Franklin Roosevelt onward believed that the United States, with its "revolutionary" heritage, was the natural ally of peoples struggling against colonialism; we could win the allegiance of these new nations by opposing and occasionally undermining our European allies in the areas of their colonial dominance. Churchill, of course, resisted these American pressures, as did the French and some other European powers for a longer period than did Britain.

As Europe decolonized, partly under American pressure, there began a reversal of roles, the march by each side toward the philosophical positions vacated by the other — to an America focused on international security and a Europe affirming general moral precepts of conduct. On Third World issues especially, many in Europe have ended up adopting the attitude embodied in Roosevelt's anticolonialism and Eisenhower's conduct over Suez. Now Europe would seek to identify with Third World aspirations, economic and political, intensifying its efforts at conciliation the more insistent, peremptory, and radical that Third World demands become. At the same time, the United States, at least in some administrations, has come to a perception closer to Eden's: that appeasement of radical challenges only multiplies radical challenges.

Different perceptions of national interest were involved as well. Thus in the India-Pakistan war of 1971 Britain did not share our sense of concern for the country which had opened the first tenuous links to China; the historic nostalgia for India was too strong. So too in the early stages of the Falkland crisis America hesitated between its Atlantic and its Western hemisphere vocations. But neither of these disagreements did any lasting damage. In the end we came together; the old friendship prevailed over the other considerations.

The lesson I draw is that in the Third World we may occasionally operate from different perspectives. But we must take care not to let these differences reach a point where they undermine the basic self-confidence and sense of mission of the other party, lest we threaten prospects for progress and stability transcending the immediate issue.

In this context the experience of Suez is instructive. Our prolonged and never-reconciled clash had lasting consequences not only for the Middle East and the Third World but also for the long-term evolution of Western policies.

The details of that disaster are not relevant to my immediate purpose. The British-French expedition against the Suez Canal was clearly misconceived. The fact remains that Eden had got hold of what was intellectually the right problem, while the American reaction, among other things, begged some crucial questions: to what extent our "revolutionary" historical analogy was relevant; to what extent it was wise to humiliate one's closest ally; and what would be the long-term consequence of such a course.

Britain and France, in my view, were acting on a strategic analysis which may have been traditional and even self-serving but was far from frivolous. Nasser was the first Third World leader to accept Soviet arms and to play the radical, pro-Soviet game in an attempt to blackmail the West. Eden's perception was that a dangerous precedent was being set: can there be any dispute of this today? Had Nasser's course been shown a failure, a quite different pattern of international relations would have developed, at least for a decade or more. As it turned out, Nasser's policy was vindicated; revolutions spread in the Middle East in the following years, and he has countless imitators today around the world relying on Soviet arms to increase their influence and to destabilize their neighbors.

Even more important, our humiliation of Britain and France over Suez was a shattering blow to these countries' role as world powers. It accelerated their shedding of international responsibilities, some of the consequences of which we saw in succeeding decades when reality forced *us* to step into their shoes — in the Persian Gulf, to take one notable example. Suez thus added enormously to America's burdens — and simultaneously fueled a European resentment at America's global role which continues to this day.

It is clear that a world of progress and peace requires that more than one hundred new and developing nations be made part of the international system; no international order can survive unless they feel a stake in it. It is incontestable that many conflicts in the developing world arise from legitimate social, economic, or political grievances; this, however, does not exclude the possibility that these can be exploited by extremists and turned against the long-term security interests of the West. The democracies, whatever their shifting positions, have failed to relate their philosophical and moral convictions to a co-

herent analysis of the nature of revolution and an understanding of
how best to foster moderation. Above all, disputes among the democracies over this problem should not be permitted to turn into a kind of
guerrilla warfare between allies. Whatever the merit of the individual
issue, the price will be a weakening of the West's overall psychological readiness to maintain the global balance.

The strategic position or self-confidence of a close ally on a matter it considers of vital concern must not be undermined. It is a principle of no little contemporary relevance. In this sense the Falkland
crisis in the end will strengthen Western cohesion.

Suez, by weakening Europe's sense of its own importance as a
world power, accelerated the trend of Europe's seeking refuge in the
role of "mediator" between the United States and the Soviet Union.
The role that some American leaders naively saw the United States as
playing between Churchill and Stalin, in the end too many Europeans
seek to adopt between Washington and Moscow.

It is not a new phenomenon. It began, at least where Britain was
involved, as wise advice to us that negotiation could be an element of
strategy. This is a lesson of which Americans often need to be re-
minded. It has its antecedents in Attlee's flight to Washington for re-
assurance when Truman seemed to hint at using nuclear weapons in
Korea; in Eden's efforts at various Geneva conferences to sponsor a
dialogue in the era of Dulles's moralism; in Macmillan's appearance in
an astrakhan hat in Moscow in 1959; in the strenuous Western European importunings of the Nixon Administration in 1969 to join Europe in the pursuit of détente. But carried too far, it runs the risk of
abdicating any share of responsibility for a cohesive Western strategy
toward the USSR, or toward anti-Western radicalism in the Third
World.

And thus we see the ironic shift of positions reflected in some of
our contemporary debates. The deprecation of the importance of
power, the abstract faith in goodwill, the belief in the pacific efficacy
of economic relations, the evasion of the necessities of defense and
security, the attempt to escape from the sordid details of maintaining
the global balance of power, the presumption of superior morality —
these features once characteristic of America now seem to be more

common in Europe. Where the United States has never quite abandoned its earlier moralism or fully developed a concept of equilibrium
as Europe had once maintained, many in Europe paradoxically seem
to have adopted some of the illusions that Americans clung to in years
of isolation from responsibility.

The unity of the industrial democracies remains crucial to the
survival of democratic values and of the global equilibrium. We must
at last answer the perennial questions of all alliances: How much unity
do we need? How much diversity can we stand? An insistence on unanimity can be a prescription for paralysis. But if every ally acts as it
pleases, what is the meaning of alliance? There is no more important
task before the Alliance than to deal with these problems concretely,
seriously, and above all immediately.

THE CONTEMPORARY DEBATE

Let me make a few general points, therefore, about the contemporary
debates between America and Europe.

I do not claim that the United States is always correct in its perceptions. But Europeans ought to take care not to generate such frustrations in America that either an embittered nationalism, or
unilateralism, or a retreat from world affairs could result.

I fully acknowledge that the United States by its actions has
sometimes stimulated or intensified the feelings in Europe that Europe had to strive to maintain its own interests, its own policies, its
own identity. Indeed, as I said, naive American expectations that a
rejuvenated Europe would follow our lead are partly responsible for
the sometimes petulant reaction to Europe's assertions of its own
role. In recent times the United States may have appeared uninten-
tionally callous toward the danger of nuclear war or insufficiently alert
to the opportunities for peace. But the United States has nevertheless
been more nearly correct than its critics in warning that those who
seek peace not backed by strength will sooner or later find the terms
of peace dictated to them; that peace to be meaningful must be just;

that nations live in history, not utopia, and thus must approach their goals in stages. To ask for perfection as a precondition of action is self-indulgence, and in the end an abdication.

Observers, including myself, have been sounding the alarm for decades about this or that "crisis" in the Western Alliance. But today's, I am afraid, is more genuinely, objectively, serious than ever. It comes after decades of a relentless Soviet military buildup, when the West, for a decade, is edging in some areas toward a dangerous dependency on economic ties with the East; while in Poland the So-viet Union enforces the unity of its empire, its clients press on to un-dermine the security interests of the West from Southeast Asia to the Middle East to Africa to Central America. Not all our difficulties are caused by the Soviet Union, but the Soviet Union has shown little re-straint in exploiting them, and their solution — whatever their cause — has been impeded by the lack of a unified Western response.

One of Britain's contributions to the Western Alliance has been to supply a needed global perspective: the knowledge, from centuries of experience in Europe, that peace requires some clear-eyed notion of equilibrium and a willingness to maintain it; the insight, from cen-turies of world leadership, that Europe's security cannot be isolated from the broader context of the global balance; the awareness, from heroic exertions in this century, that those who cherish the values of Western civilization must be willing to defend them. In the Falkland crisis, Britain is reminding us all that certain basic principles such as honor, justice, and patriotism remain valid and must be sustained by more than words.

The issue before the allies now is not to assess blame but to face our future. An alliance at odds over central issues of East-West diplo-macy, economic policy, the Middle East, Central America, Africa, and relations with the Third World is in serious, and obvious, difficulty. Indeed, it cannot be called an alliance if it agrees on *no* significant issue. Sooner or later such divisions *must* affect the field of security. For too long, all of us in the community of free nations have put off the uncomfortable questions; our evasions are now coming home to roost.

Thirty-five years ago, after the war, the democracies for a time overestimated the immediate dangers and underestimated their own capabilities; yet in the end they came up with a creative and effective response. Today, too, we may be underrating our own capacities and confusing long- and short-term dangers.

The strange aspect is that the disarray is taking place at the precise moment that the bankruptcy of the system that denies the human spirit seems to become clear beyond doubt. The Communist world has fundamental systemic problems and has not shown any ability to solve them except by recurrent brute force, which only delays the day of reckoning. In the sixty-five-year history of the Soviet state, it has never managed a legitimate, regular succession of its political leadership; the country faces the demographic time bomb of its growing non-Russian population, soon to be a majority. The system has failed to deal seriously with the desire for political participation of its intellectual and managerial elite. Or else it has sought to preempt their political aspirations by turning the ruling group into a careerist "new class" bound to produce stagnation if not corruption. Its ideology is a discredited failure, without legitimacy, leaving the Communist party a smug, privileged elite with no function in the society except its own self-perpetuation, struggling to deal with bottlenecks and crises which its own rigidity has caused. It is an historic joke that the ultimate crisis in every Communist state, latent if not evident, is over the role of the Communist party.

Soviet economic performance is a disaster. It seems impossible to run a modern economy by a system of total planning, yet it seems impossible to maintain a Communist state *without* a system of total planning. How ironic that the West is tearing itself apart over how best to coordinate Western financial, technological, and agricultural *aid* to a so-called superpower incapable of sustaining a modern economy!

In short, if Moscow is prevented by a coordinated Western policy from deflecting its internal tensions into international crises, it is likely to find only disillusionment in the boast that history is on its side.

It is the Communist world, not the West, that faces a profound systemic crisis. Ours are problems of coordination and policy, theirs are of structure. And therefore it is not beyond the realm of hope that a coherent, unified Western policy could at long last bring into view the prospect of a negotiated global settlement that Churchill foresaw at Llandudno.

The solutions to the West's problems are, to a significant degree, in our own hands.

One problem is that the democracies have no forum for addressing the future in a concrete way, let alone harmonizing disagreements or implementing common policies. As my friend Christopher Soames has recently emphasized, the Atlantic Alliance has no institutional machinery for addressing economic or Third World issues, or any long-term political strategy; the European Community, while eminently successful in its political coordination, has no mechanism as yet for formulating a coherent European view on matters of defense. The economic summits of Western and Japanese leaders, begun in the mid-1970s, are an attempt to surmount this procedural impasse, but they can do little more than call key leaders' attention to key problems in an informal, unsystematic way. Procedures do not solve substantive problems. Nevertheless, creating an appropriate forum for broader and deeper consultation would be an important first step.

America has learned much in the postwar period, perhaps most of all from Britain. In the last decade we have also learned something of our limits, and in the new Administration we have shaken off the trauma of perhaps excessive preoccupation with those limits. An America that has recovered its vitality and its faith in the future is as much in the interests of the West as a Europe shaping its identity.

Both Britain and America have learned that whatever their histories, their futures are part of the common destiny of freedom. Experience has taught that moral idealism and geopolitical insight are not alternatives but complementary; our civilization may not survive unless we possess *both* in full measure. Britain and America, which have contributed so much to the free world's unity and strength, have another opportunity now, together with our allies, to show that the democratic nations are the masters of their destiny.

STRATEGY, TRADE, AND THE ATLANTIC ALLIANCE

Extracts from an address inaugurating the Geri Joseph Lectureship on Public Affairs, Nieuwe Kerk, The Hague, May 12, 1982

THE MOMENT is appropriate for dialogue because the Alliance of the democracies is in grave difficulty. A new generation on both sides of the Atlantic has no personal memory of the crises and dangers which gave birth to that Alliance. It takes for granted the achievements which have produced nearly four decades of peace in Europe and, despite all current difficulties, unprecedented prosperity. That tradition of unity must be nurtured. If the democracies fail to stand together in a world increasingly inhospitable to democracy and liberty, they will first lose the coherence of their policies and ultimately their freedom.

The Atlantic Alliance has unfortunately been living off capital for too long. Alliance obligations have never required unanimity; up to a point, free peoples should be able to translate diversity into creativity. But we are no longer dealing with only occasional disagreements. There is almost no issue on which the allies are in accord — whether it is nuclear strategy, political and economic relations with the Soviet Union, Central America, or the Middle East. That situation cannot continue without impairing the security relationship which has maintained the peace in Europe and the world for a generation.

I am not here as a spokesman for the American Administration or for any of its particular policies. To be sure, many of its members are friends and former colleagues, and I speak with some understanding of their dilemmas and considerable sympathy for their aspirations. I am here as a private citizen who has always believed passionately in the political and moral importance of the Alliance of the democracies. In this spirit, I want to discuss two of the key problems in the European-American debate: nuclear weapons, and economic relations with the Soviet Union.

THE PROBLEM OF NUCLEAR WEAPONS

That nuclear weapons have added a new dimension to warfare and indeed human existence, that they make obsolete traditional concepts of military victory, that they stake civilized life and perhaps humanity itself, is not a new discovery. Some of us have been warning for over two decades that excessive reliance on nuclear weapons would sooner or later lead to the psychological paralysis of Western defense strategy. Where we differed from much of the current agitation is in our rejection of unilateralism. We drew the conclusion that reducing dependence on nuclear weapons obliged us to seek alternative means of defense, especially a buildup of conventional forces. The democracies' desire for peace must not be allowed to turn into a weapon of blackmail in the hands of the most ruthless.

In too many NATO countries, protests and mass demonstrations against nuclear weapons tend inevitably toward a unilateral psychological, and even physical, disarmament with respect to the very weapons upon which Western security has in fact depended. The impression is created that it is the Alliance's possession of nuclear arms — weapons which it did not use when it had an atomic monopoly and overwhelming superiority — which threatens the peace and which must be resisted. Little attention is paid to a whole series of aggressive or intransigent Soviet actions, from the dispatch of Cuban troops to Africa through the occupation of Afghanistan to the repression of freedom in Poland, which not only threatened the global equilibrium but were the proximate cause of the breakdown of strategic arms control negotiations in the 1970s.

Even less attention is paid to some basic facts of postwar history: that but for Soviet pressures in the immediate postwar period American troops would have been withdrawn from Europe in the forties, as indeed they were from Korea; that but for the Korean war the US military budget would have shrunk to derisory levels; that it was the threat to the freedom of Berlin in the late fifties which accelerated the American military buildup; that the Soviet strategic arsenal has grown and been modernized relentlessly since the Cuban missile crisis twenty years ago; that for a variety of reasons the United States stopped its numerical buildup in the late sixties and slowed its modernization for the better part of the seventies; and that *all* wars in the postwar period have started where there were *no* American forces and *no* nuclear weapons, while Europe under American nuclear protection has enjoyed the longest period of peace in its history.

For all these reasons, the clamor for peace in much of the West is in most respects addressed to the wrong governments. Unmatched as it is by comparable agitation in the East, it poses the danger that a psychological imbalance, indeed a form of unilateral disarmament, will compound the regional military imbalances which have already produced such a sense of insecurity in almost all countries around the periphery of the Soviet Union.

And yet the moral concern about nuclear weapons touches upon an issue crucial to our future: mankind's newfound ability to exterminate itself makes new modes of thinking imperative. But they do not require a flight from concreteness; hysteria is a poor guide to policy. Moral concern must be coupled with a willingness to think through the central issues with a seriousness and in a detail that do justice to dangers as complex as they are enormous.

All consideration of the nuclear question must begin with this reality: tens of thousands of nuclear weapons have been produced by the superpowers; hundreds by medium-sized countries; dozens by recent and possibly new entrants into the nuclear club. No scheme of disarmament could account for all these weapons. Nations would insist on residual forces to protect themselves against cheating, or against the fact that the factories that produced the weapons would remain, or, should by some improbable chance these too be destroyed, against the knowledge in the minds of men from which these factories and weapons sprang in the first place. Mankind cannot unlearn the secret of the atom. In other words, we are doomed to some kind of deterrence, equilibrium, or balance at some level and in some form.

For the immediate future — even assuming foreseeable reductions — that level will be quite high; the real issue before us will be the nature of deterrence, and its components. That problem is neither new nor the exclusive discovery of newly concerned groups in all our countries. Technology would have imposed a reconsideration of existing strategy in any event; the destructiveness of weapons was bound sooner or later to break the cocoon in which we suppressed the consciousness of our Promethean power. But the public outcry has had the healthy result of forcing governments into considerations that they should in fact have initiated; of coming to grips with the awesomeness of the choices into which they have slid because of their reluctance to face, and tell their publics, the implications of their own design.

Our current dilemmas are the result of the decision of all our postwar leaders to base security on technology — to compensate for an assumed Soviet superiority in manpower and conventional weapons by reliance on our nuclear arsenal. Stalin's aggressiveness was real enough. But from the perspective of a generation, it is possible to argue that the West was too ready to attribute a military edge to an adversary only recently devastated by war and 20 million casualties; that the NATO nations underestimated the significance of their own industrial potential and forgot — conveniently — that in fact NATO's manpower is greater than that of the East. All these reflections are now academic. For the immediate future, the West is locked into the decisions of a generation; whatever conclusions we draw from the current realities and the concerns they generate, for at least a transitional period it will be nuclear weapons which inhibit aggression in Europe. The evasions of three decades cannot be remedied by proclamations but only by hard and dedicated effort.

The principal evasion was the refusal to face the fact that strategic nuclear weapons could continue to counterbalance local Soviet advantages only if the US strategic arsenal was clearly superior to that of the Soviet Union — superiority being defined as the ability to destroy the opposing nuclear capability at acceptable cost. That condition began to disappear in the sixties. Technology tended toward equality, and to levels beyond which additional increments of destructiveness lose all relationship to the objectives likely to be in dispute. Under current conditions superiority to be meaningful would require an edge so large that no opponent would tolerate it and calculations so esoteric that few leaders will understand them or stake survival on them. Arms control theory and practice, with their formal emphasis on equality, only accelerated and legitimized this trend.

While all these changes were taking place Western governments and societies preferred to ignore the consequences of their own decisions. Logically, once the Soviet Union acquired the capacity to threaten the United States with direct nuclear retaliation, the American pledge to launch an all-out nuclear war on behalf of Europe was bound increasingly to lose its credibility and public acceptance, if not its sense — and so would the Alliance's defense strategy. For the strategy now rested on the threat to initiate mutual suicide. But governments continued the existing strategy, seeking to compensate by emphatic reiterations of all-out nuclear defense for the implausibility of their professions.

I made these points in a speech in Brussels in the fall of 1979; I was roundly criticized for allegedly undermining the credibility of NATO strategy. Unfortunately, what I said was true and has now come to pass. For more than two decades it was obvious that US–Soviet nuclear parity would lead us — sooner or later — to this point. And for more than two decades, the West has hid its head in the sand and ignored the inevitable.

There was an occasional flirtation with a doctrine of limited nuclear war to restore some relationship between policy and military power. In my early writings on the subject in the 1950s, I, too, was briefly tempted by that theory. The effort never got very far. Part of the reason was that from the European perspective, the distinction between limited and general nuclear war was not as clear-cut as on the American side of the Atlantic; a relatively few nuclear weapons could produce catastrophe and chaos difficult to distinguish from what only total war could do to America. Another cause was the polarization within the community of civilian experts between those who wanted to make nuclear weapons "conventional" and those who feared that governments could be kept from initiating a nuclear holocaust only by guaranteeing that nuclear war would be as gruesome as possible. Ironically, those circles usually advocating humane and progressive domestic policies generally *insisted* that nuclear strategy be aimed primarily at the mass extermination of civilians.

I continue to believe that in practice governments will be more careful than in their concepts. Indeed, it is reckless in a nuclear world to pretend that any accident must automatically escalate into Armageddon. I hope that if the worst happens, governments *will* seek limits to the use of nuclear weapons — they will almost surely find them. Still, in all likelihood, the problem of limiting the use of weapons whose power has no operationally definable limit will find no acceptable consensus in advance; as a practical matter, failure to achieve a consensus over a period of thirty years is a pretty good working definition of the impossibility of developing in the abstract a strategy of limited nuclear war.

Unfortunately, many who opposed theories of limited nuclear war recoiled as well before the conventional military buildup which could have at least reduced or perhaps avoided altogether the local and regional Soviet superiority that gave rise to the reliance on nuclear weapons in the first place. The legacy we are left with is a precarious combination of a NATO reliance on nuclear defense, trends toward nuclear stalemate, growing nuclear pacifism, and continued deficiencies in conventional forces. If we are reluctant to resort to nuclear weapons, and if we continue to evade the necessity for conventional forces, the Western Alliance is left with no defense policy at all, and we are risking the collapse of the military balance in Europe that has made possible thirty-five years of European security, prosperity, and democracy. We will in effect have disarmed ourselves unilaterally while sitting on the most destructive stockpile of weapons that the world has seen.

*   *   *

RENOUNCING THE FIRST USE OF NUCLEAR WEAPONS

The issue of the intermediate-range missiles is a symptom, not a cause, of the current malaise over strategy. The real issue remains the need to gear our defense policies to the twin realities of strategic parity and mounting public concern over nuclear weapons. Recently a serious proposal to that end was made by a group of eminent Americans: Robert McNamara, McGeorge Bundy, George Kennan, and Gerard Smith, all of whom have held high office. Among other things, the views of these outstanding public servants should serve as a reminder to our European friends that if frustration reaches a certain point, American policy could shift drastically away from the now dominant trend.

I greatly respect these men, who advanced the thesis that NATO should renounce the first use of nuclear weapons and rely exclusively on conventional weapons for the defense of Europe — and *a fortiori* of other threatened areas. I share their objective that the West must disenthrall itself of the notion that it can substitute technology for sacrifice and destructiveness for effort. I cannot, however, agree with their declaratory policy, for four principal reasons:

A statement of no first use would leave us psychologically naked in the intermediate period that would surely extend over at least five years, even if our own government and all our NATO allies were prepared to make immediate, serious, and sustained efforts to redress the imbalance in conventional weapons. Of course, if the reaction of our allies were less enthusiastic about conventional rearmament than anticipated by the authors, the psychological and military vulnerability of NATO would be magnified even more. Our leaders have an obligation to reduce their reliance on nuclear weapons; they must not do so, however, at the price of accelerating a trend of pacifism and panic that may invite Soviet nuclear blackmail. Much of the antinuclear agitation is, after all, directed against the West's nonnuclear weapons as well.

A formal pledge of no first use may well create, in addition, two seemingly contradictory dangers which increase the risk of war. If the Soviets should become convinced that the West fears nuclear war above all else, we may trigger one of the not infrequent reversals of Soviet strategic doctrine, from hints of abjuring first use to the reassertion that a war in Europe could never be limited to conventional weapons. All wars, it would then be argued (as at times it has in the past) will be nuclear — facing the West with the choice of surrender or the kind of war of which our countries will then be incapable as a result of years of renouncing and stigmatizing nuclear weapons.

Nor can we afford to create the impression that we would prefer a conventional defeat in Europe to the first use of nuclear weapons. The history of conventional warfare is filled with examples of battles in which numbers and equipment were roughly equal and yet victory was achieved by such unquantifiable factors as superior tactics, superior strategy, or superior leadership. For centuries wars have started between seemingly evenly matched forces. There is no blinking the fact that deterrence, when only conventional weapons were involved, has frequently broken down. And we probably could then not guarantee that we would live up to our no-first-use declaration. Faced with the collapse of Europe we might well reverse our proclaimed doctrine, thereby bringing about the worst of all possible outcomes: a failure of conventional deterrence *and* a nuclear war.

Finally, a no-first-use declaration would likely demoralize allies in other regions of the world or other friendly countries, large and small, not embraced by formal alliances and yet as dependent on American strength as they are vital to Western security.

With all these caveats, the authors of the no-first-use proposal have rendered an important service. While I cannot accept their prescription, they have correctly grasped the key challenge: as they point out, the West has no choice but to give greater priority to its conventional defense. As a practical matter, it *must* be our policy to reduce reliance on nuclear war to the greatest extent possible, by creating other means to resist aggression.

This requires more than exhortations, however. The United States has abolished the draft; most of our allies have reduced their terms of compulsory military service; everywhere military budgets are under pressure from increasingly insistent social demands. If we are serious about seeking to reduce the danger of nuclear weapons, we must be serious as well about military efforts in the conventional field, and must face up to the question of the adequacy of our military budgets and volunteer armies.

STRATEGIC ARMS LIMITATION AND REDUCTION

It has been NATO policy since at least the Harmel Report of 1967 that the Atlantic Alliance has two main functions: to maintain the collective defense, and to seek a more stable relationship with the East by willingness to resolve political problems through negotiations. Arms control has had a crucial role in this effort. Public support for defense and for resistance to Soviet challenges can be sustained in the democracies only by demonstrating that the West is not the cause of confrontations. We have seen in recent years that failure to observe this maxim generates massive pressure groups that then exact perhaps excessive concessions from governments belatedly recognizing their impact and suddenly eager to placate them.

To be effective, arms control must be seen as a component of security policy. Experience shows that it can ratify or stabilize a military balance, not serve as a substitute for it. Indeed, it is the stable military balance in Europe that has made possible several decades of efforts to ease tensions with the Soviet Union. If arms control comes to be perceived primarily as an exercise in moral virtue — because either advocates turn demagogic or governments self-indulgent — it becomes a form of self-paralysis. The premise of arms control must be that security can be enhanced if the balance is maintained at lower, agreed, and verifiable levels of forces.

This is why so much hope has been attached for over a decade to US–Soviet talks on stragetic arms control and why President Reagan has reaffirmed the commitment of all of his predecessors to limiting these weapons of mass destruction, giving special emphasis to reductions. And that is why there have emerged the various freeze proposals now under active discussion in the United States.

President Reagan's commitment to strategic arms talks marks a watershed in the American domestic debate. For nearly a decade, disputes over strategic weapons limitation have torn our domestic consensus, becoming symbolic surrogates for larger controversies over policy toward the Soviet Union. Arms control negotiations over the years have been buffeted by debates between competing philosophies sometimes only indirectly touching upon the details being negotiated. Advocates have made exorbitant claims and insisted on separating arms control from all other aspects of policy; opponents saw in them a serious weakening of Western willpower and concentrated on portraying the inherent balancing of relative advantages as unilateral concessions. President Reagan, by proposing and entering a negotiation over strategic arms reduction, will have liberated our domestic debate and permitted a serious public discussion of the real issues of arms control. The delay in starting the talks, legitimately needed for preparation, is a small price to pay for opening up prospects of a successful conclusion that were not available to either of his two immediate predecessors.

There exists, then, an unprecedented opportunity. Frustration with the apparent slow pace of diplomacy and the desire for a dramatic breakthrough have produced various proposals for nuclear freezes. Experience has shown, however, that it is easy to formulate general objectives in arms control negotiations; it is much more difficult to negotiate a meaningful outcome whatever principle is finally adopted. We have, after all, the experience of the two SALT agreements which were both essentially a kind of numerical freeze. Complex negotiations went on for years over what weapons to count; how to relate multiple warheads to individual delivery vehicles; and how to relate either to airborne weapons of mass destruction. Attempting a freeze now would encounter all the old SALT dilemmas — for example, of where to draw the dividing line between "modernized" and "new" systems. Who can forget the Soviets' attempt to define all of their replacement weapons as only "modernized" and hence permitted, while all of ours were said to be "new" and hence proscribed? In short, a freeze requires a baseline; by itself it is no advance over the results of the SALT process which already exists.

The Administration, in an important speech by President Reagan last Sunday [May 9, 1982], has countered by proposing a strategic arms control scheme based on reductions. This surely addresses the concerns of many who express unhappiness at the scale of nuclear arsenals. And the Administration is also dealing with what is the real heart of the matter, namely crisis stability, or diminishing the danger of the outbreak of nuclear war. For if the reductions are merely numerical, without concern for the composition and nature of strategic forces, they could increase instability rather than ease it. After all, the overwhelming new problem in the strategic field is the existence of multiple warheads on strategic missiles. Even if the launchers on both sides are exactly equal, the disproportion between the number of attacking warheads and the number of launcher/targets represents a standing temptation to strike first. Reductions do not automatically change the disproportion. In fact, at some levels reducing the number of missiles without changing the proportion of warheads to missiles increases the vulnerability of the missiles attacked; a first strike is simplified. The Reagan Administration is surely on the right track in striving for a proposal that combines reductions with restrictions on other characteristics of weapons to inhibit, rather than ease, a surprise attack.

But it is also true that such a process is enormously time-consuming, not only in elaborating our own position but in negotiating an agreement with the Soviet Union. It took years of SALT negotiations to agree on numerical limits on launchers; the negotiations now envisaged are infinitely more complex.

The gap must be bridged. There is an urgent need to demonstrate to our publics that both sides are serious about getting the arms race under control. Otherwise careless "quick-fix" solutions are likely to dominate the field. In my view, the existing SALT framework may be useful in providing the baselines from which to negotiate over the complex reductions that our Administration is in the process of developing. At the same time, we must take seriously the concerns expressed in the Senate debate on ratification of SALT II. On that occasion, I supported ratification if three conditions were fulfilled: first, if a major defense buildup were undertaken to restore the military balance; second, if certain amendments were made and if specific ambiguities, particularly in the accompanying three-year Protocol, were cleared up; and third, if the United States made clear the linkage between SALT and Soviet geopolitical conduct. Some senators, led by the then minority leader Senator Howard Baker, stressed the importance of maintaining the American right to build heavy ICBMs such as the Soviet Union already possessed in large numbers.

These are valid concerns, and I believe that we are at a stage where they can be met. The Reagan Administration's rearmament effort will in time balance the Soviet buildup; it is urgently needed — but in any case, the Administration has voluntarily kept it within SALT II limits. The Protocol has been overtaken by the passage of time. (The interval foreseen for it is ending in any case.) We could therefore proceed to an interim agreement using the SALT framework or, as some former opponents of the treaty such as Senator Sam Nunn have indicated, ratify the SALT II treaty. I would lean to that course, with the following additions to the existing SALT framework:

• First, spelling out an American right to build heavy ICBMs equivalent to the Soviets'. My impression is that the MX, which is permitted under the treaty, meets all current American objectives (and also that it raises enough problems of deployment in its own right). It is therefore unlikely that we would build an even heavier missile. Still, a treaty that deprives the United States of the formal right to aim for equivalence with the Soviets raises serious problems of equity. Alternatively, we could offer to trade reductions or even elimination of the MX for similar restraints on the Soviet heavy missile, the SS-18.

• Second, lowering the ceilings below the limits established by SALT II to around 2,000–2,100 strategic delivery vehicles. This would symbolize a commitment to reductions.

• Third, extending the agreement's duration to 1987, instead of 1985 — to be superseded by a reduction agreement, of course, if concluded earlier. This would provide time for the agreement to be reflected in the weapons decisions of the parties and a sense of security for the comprehensive reductions and qualitative restrictions our Administration is properly seeking.

Reverting to the framework of SALT II as a point of departure for an interim period may seem to some to reopen partisan wounds. The answer is that the Reagan Administration is in fact observing the numerical limits agreed in SALT II. I have great difficulty understanding why it is safe to adhere to a nonratified agreement while it is unsafe formally to ratify what one is already observing. The Soviets may in fact prefer such a posture, all the more so as nonratification gives them at least 250 extra delivery vehicles which they would be obliged to destroy by the terms of the treaty once ratified.

I stress that these are the ideas of a private American who on this subject has had next to no access to Administration thinking. But it seems to me a responsible way to end the current impasse, establish a baseline for later reductions, and end the agitation for quick fixes reflecting more passion than analysis.

But no step forward toward arms control will advance us decisively toward a stable peace unless we are willing to confront two corollaries. First, we must always keep in mind that any agreement on limiting or reducing strategic weapons will further undermine the credibility of a strategy based on their use. It thus reemphasizes the urgent need to redress the imbalance in conventional forces. Western governments must not use an agreement as an excuse to slacken their defense effort but to redirect it. Or else SALT, or START, or any other acronym, will multiply our perils. We should be prepared to pay the price of a further conventional buildup; we must not pretend that there is no price.

Second, important as arms control is, commitment to it must not obscure the basic reality: as a general principle arms do not cause political tensions; they reflect them. It cannot be in the interest of the West to permit the Soviet Union to use arms control talks as a safety valve to avoid the consequences of aggressive behavior. In the past decade, almost every Soviet aggressive move has been followed by an offer to accelerate arms talks. In the long run, the Soviets may be misled into believing that they can safely challenge the global balance and escape the consequences by conciliatory rhetoric. Even as we insulate arms talks to some degree from political discussions, we must never forget that the cause of tensions is the political conflict between East and West, the clash of philosophies and the Soviet effort to expand its power and its sphere. Sooner or later there must be a settlement of this political conflict or all subsidiary negotiations will ultimately become irrelevancies.

Thus, the deeper challenge to Western leaders is whether they are willing to face complexity; whether they can educate their peoples to the knowledge that passion can give an impetus but only analysis can produce results, that arms control cannot survive in conditions of permanent geopolitical challenge: whether, in short, the democracies can muster the discipline and the cohesion for facing their perils with a sense of purpose instead of running from them in confusion and division.

ECONOMIC RELATIONS WITH THE SOVIET UNION

The Allied disputes over security have had their origin in European initiatives; those over East-West trade have received their impetus from America. Two successive American administrations have vainly sought European support to restrict East-West trade by proscribing the sale of certain commodities or interrupting long-term projects such as the gas pipeline, first over the Soviet invasion of Afghanistan, then over the suppression of liberty in Poland. The resulting disagreements have left an unfortunate residue: in America, many believe that our European allies subordinate long-term strategy and even security to short-term domestic politics; in Europe, many argue that America seeks to play for geopolitical stakes with European chips, risking the domestic cohesion of friendly countries over issues with respect to which we ourselves are not prepared to make equivalent sacrifices, as the lifting of our grain embargo suggests.

Let me make a few observations.

Pressures for East-West trade grew in the late sixties and early seventies — ironically in the wake of the Soviet invasion of Czechoslovakia. It was argued in some quarters that despite occasional Soviet transgressions, increased East-West trade would moderate Soviet behavior by making the USSR increasingly dependent on the technology and grain of the industrial democracies. The American Administration then in office, in which I served, held from the first that trade should *follow* prior demonstrations of Soviet commitment to a more peaceful course and should be linked to Soviet international behavior. When the Soviet Union entered into serious negotiations on Berlin, SALT, mutual force reductions and other matters, the United States gradually lifted restrictions, on a case-by-case basis and tied to specific projects. Our European allies followed in our wake and, when congressional restrictions intervened, far surpassed us in both the scale of their trade and credit and the ease with which they made it available.

Whatever the merit of the original theories, it is now clearly demonstrated that trade and credits can moderate Soviet conduct only if the Kremlin fears that intransigence will cost it the economic benefits it seeks. Yet that is what is most insistently rejected by the domestic interest groups in all countries which gain from East-West trade and by the Western governments which they influence. More and more, the governments of the industrial democracies act on the premise that the immediate gains in employment outweigh the political risks in strengthening a hostile and aggressive political system. This is all the more shortsighted, as a mounting tide of radicalism and insecurity in the world — the inevitable consequence of a growth of Soviet power unrestrained by some agreed code of conduct — will sooner or later compound all economic difficulties as well.

There is little doubt that over the past decade the negotiating balance in East-West trade has been reversed. In every crisis, the West invents new excuses for why it would be inappropriate to interrupt economic relations, including the totally contradictory propositions that "sanctions never work" and "sanctions are tantamount to an act of war" — the last an especially dangerous legitimization of Soviet blackmail should economic sanctions ever prove unavoidable. Economic relations, indeed, have done much more to induce *Western* restraint in the face of Soviet misconduct than to encourage Soviet restraint in its international behavior.

The inequality in bargaining positions is almost entirely the result of the disunity of the democracies. Theoretically, trade occurs only when it is to the mutual benefit of both sides. But the division of the benefits is the subject of bargaining; overdependence on one market or one seller tilts the balance, especially when a centrally directed system faces a group of countries competing with each other. This is precisely what is happening in East-West trade. The USSR deals with its opposite numbers in the West through a purchasing commission, a single unit subject to strict political direction. The West is divided into competing units sometimes prevented by antitrust legislation from acting together and often encouraged by national governments which seek special benefits for their national industries by concessional credits. Loans have been offered or encouraged with little or no consideration of Soviet or East European ability to use or repay the funds. Default is avoided by "rescheduling," that is, lending more money to pay interest on what are in effect bad loans — protecting the lenders' balance sheet. In these circumstances it is easy for the Kremlin to play off the Western countries, and even industries, against each other, obtaining benefits not justified by the economic balance of advantage, much less by political circumstances. Against all traditional expectations the "debtor's" bargaining position improves with his inability to repay his debts.

The result has been an anomaly. By any objective analysis, the Soviet Union and its satellites are infinitely more dependent on East-West trade than their trading partners, the industrial democracies. The Soviet Union cannot feed itself without the non-Communist world's grain; it desperately needs Western technology. The typical Western product for sale in the East contains new ideas; what the Soviet Union has to offer in return is raw materials — products which contain no conceptual input. The inequality in benefits would long since have reduced trade to a trickle had not Western governments stepped in with direct or hidden credits, which now amount to nearly $90 billion for the Communist world. In addition, many export prices are subsidized by governments directly or indirectly. The Communist countries thus are not only gaining a relative advantage in trade but also are being financed by the nations against whom they are simultaneously conducting a geopolitical offensive. Lenin's dictum that capitalists would compete to sell the rope with which they are to be hanged is coming true with a vengeance — for Lenin never guessed that Western governments would provide the money to buy the rope and subsidize the price to facilitate the purchase.

It is unthinkable that the West should continue to use its overwhelming share of the world's economic power so frivolously. We are on the defensive not because we lack resources but because we have failed to muster the will or the leadership to organize a coherent response. We have tried stop-and-go sanctions. They have failed because they affected various countries and different sectors of the economy unequally. And it was difficult to relate them to a concrete political program or to determine under what circumstances they might be ended. They have turned into pinpricks dramatizing the West's weakness rather than its mastery of the situation.

The issue has further been clouded by the extreme manner in which the choices have been stated. Some opponents of East-West trade intimate that a total denial of economic benefits will force the collapse of the Soviet system. This theory is disproved by history. The Soviet system survived several decades of economic isolation and did not crumble. And it runs counter to the domestic pressures for seeking negotiations on a broad front. The last eighteen months show that the Alliance will not sustain a policy of confrontation for its own sake unrelieved by any hope of diplomatic progress.

But the opposite theory, of the automatic mellowing effect of trade, has also been demonstrated to be fallacious. Soviet behavior in recent years has given the lie to the argument that trade and credits by themselves will bring about the benign evolution of the Soviet system. Soviet-Cuban intervention in Angola, in Ethiopia, and in South Yemen; the invasion of Afghanistan; the suppression of Solidarity in Poland; and the use of toxic chemical and biological warfare in Afghanistan and Southeast Asia have all occurred in precisely the period of expanded East-West economic cooperation.

If the democracies continue to make available their hard-earned resources for an assault on the geopolitical balance, they must not be surprised at the inevitable decline in their security and prosperity. It simply cannot be beyond the political imagination and will of the democracies to exact a penalty for intransigent and aggressive Soviet conduct. Or, to put it positively: So long as the Soviet Union asks us for help in solving its economic problems by what amounts to Western aid, the industrial democracies have the right and indeed the duty to insist on restraint and stability in international conduct in return.

The industrial democracies are in a position to use their economic strength positively and creatively. There exists a sensible rationale for East-West trade, which is neither unrestricted economic warfare nor uncontrolled Soviet access to Western trade, credit, and technology. If the democracies cannot concert unified political criteria, they should be able at least to agree on letting market conditions determine the level of East-West trade and credit. If government-guaranteed credits and subsidies were to end, East-West trade would be reduced to the level of reciprocal economic benefit — or a small fraction of what now exists. If the Soviets want to go beyond this — if they seek credits or subsidized prices — the West should insist on a *political* quid pro quo.

To this end, the industrial democracies should jointly take the position that they are prepared over the long term to engage in economic cooperation even on an augmented scale if, but only if, there is in return a comprehensive political understanding providing for settlement of the most serious outstanding problems, specific restraint in superpower conduct, and major steps toward arms reduction. The conditions should not be pious platitudes but should be spelled out in concrete detail. Nor should we delude ourselves. This cannot be achieved without a period, perhaps of some years, of disciplined coordination and restraint among the democracies to convince the Soviets that we are serious. Specifically:

• The democracies should start by clarifying and specifying their objectives in the political area to provide clear-cut criteria for progress. This could be embodied in a declaration that the West conceives its relations with the Soviet Union to go deeper than purely technical or economic exchanges. The most important message would be that the industrial democracies propose to speak with the East with one voice on economic issues and that they will demand political reciprocity for governmentally encouraged trade.

• Second, there should be an urgent review and modernization of the list of prohibited strategic exports together with a determination to stick to it.

• Third, democracies should examine at the highest level on what political terms the Soviet Union and the nations in its system will enjoy governmentally supported access to Western trade and financial resources. Policies on export credits and financial guarantees should be reviewed periodically, based on a commitment to establish a common and noncompetitive policy among all OECD members.

• Fourth, the democracies should agree to end progressively all government subsidies and guarantees for private bank credits to Eastern Europe. Given the nearly catastrophic performance of Communist economies, the marketplace would determine the proper flow of private credit, probably to restrict if not eliminate it. The same principle should apply to subsidized prices.

• Concurrently, there should be an agreement that rescheduling of existing debts will be heavily influenced by behavior of the countries concerned, especially in the field of foreign policy but including an end of martial law in Poland.

• Fifth, an urgent review of the grain export policy of the major grain-producing nations is needed to determine how it can serve the strategy sketched here without undue hardship to the farmers in all our countries.

• Finally, there must be a consensus among the democracies as to what form of expanded economic cooperation we are prepared to undertake with the Communist world if this strategy of Western economic coordination leads to a broad East-West political understanding.

The Versailles summit would seem to provide a useful forum to begin such a process of coordinating and unifying the policies of the industrial democracies.

It may be argued that these measures are utopian; that the West will never muster the discipline and mutual confidence for such a course. But what these measures suggest is in the long-term interest of both East and West. It discourages Soviet adventurism grounded in the belief that the West is too weak, too selfish, or too divided to defend its interests with its best weapons. It thus forces the Soviets to make real choices at a time when their succession struggle will inevitably involve an internal debate over priorities and a possible desire to ease outside pressures. If it leads to the sort of political settlement that precludes later reversal, trade and credit can safely be expanded. If such a settlement is unattainable, continuing our present trade and credit practices will in effect accelerate our crisis. In that case, future generations will not be able to explain what possessed their predecessors to engineer their own decline by lassitude, greed, and lack of leadership.

If the industrial democracies wish to subsidize their exports by easy credit or pricing policies, the creative area for such efforts is not in the Communist countries but in the Third World — especially among its moderate, market-oriented governments.

CONCLUSION

Existing trends may sometimes appear bleak, but let us not forget that they are the result of decisions by free societies and can therefore be reversed by free decisions. For if we use our intelligence and consider our potential, we have every reason for hope. The Soviet Union is a system with no legitimate method of succession, a stagnant economy, a demographic challenge in the growth of its non-Russian population, and ideological claims whose bankruptcy is being proven by the working class of Poland in the streets of Polish cities. The joke of history is that the only spontaneous revolutions in industrialized countries have been against Communist governments.

A system that feels so threatened by even the most elementary liberties, a system so structurally unsound and inefficient, so patently contrary to the human spirit, can prevail only by our inadequacies, not by its own efforts. The West, which over centuries has shaped a great civilization — of culture, philosophy, inventiveness, and well-being — must not now abdicate control of its own destiny to short-term calculations. Democracy requires above all clarity of thought, fortitude, and leaders willing to present the facts to their people and prepared to deal with complexity. If our problems were simple, they would long since have been solved. The statesman always faces the dilemma that he must approach his goal in stages; he is responsible not only for the best that can happen but also for the worst. Perfection will therefore elude him at each stage; demagogues have no great difficulty attacking any step by comparing it with some conjectural utopia. But democracy cannot survive if debates are driven by such attitudes. It is a disservice to serious moral concerns to pretend that there is no practical dimension, just as it falsifies practical solutions to separate them from their moral content. There is no room for self-righteousness on either side of the Atlantic or within any of our countries. Any real progress, therefore, must begin within ourselves. Our values are worth defending; our unity remains a moral as well as political necessity. If we muster that much faith and purpose, liberty will thrive and the future will be shaped by the free.

FROM LEBANON TO THE WEST BANK TO THE GULF

Published in The Washington Post, *June 16, 1982*

PERHAPS THE MOST significant aspect of the clash of the Syrian and Israeli armies on the road from Beirut to Damascus was also the least noticed: both countries had entered Lebanon to prevent the emergence on their border of a PLO [Palestine Liberation Organization] political entity or military presence. Despite strenuous avowals of its devotion to the Palestinian cause, Syria in 1976 sent its army into Lebanon to prevent a PLO victory over the Lebanese Christians and indigenous Moslems. Syria's verbal commitment to the creation of a Palestinian state did not go so far as to allow one to emerge on its borders: it feared encirclement by radical forces in power in both Iraq and Lebanon. It would fight to prevent a truly autonomous Palestinian entity.

Six years later, Israel reached the same conclusion. The PLO forces pushed south by the Syrian advance in 1976 proved intolerable to the Israelis. Whatever one's judgment of the specific pretext for the Israeli assault on the Palestinians, there can be little argument about its strategic rationale. No sovereign state can tolerate indefinitely the buildup along its borders of a military force dedicated to its destruction and implementing its objectives by periodical shellings and raids. However deep their hatred for each other, Syria and Israel were in Lebanon for the same objective: to prevent the PLO from dominating that unhappy country.

LONG-TERM CONSEQUENCES

It is important to keep this reality in mind in assessing the long-term consequences of the fighting in Lebanon. For it opens up extraordinary opportunities for a dynamic American diplomacy throughout the Middle East. It is neither desirable nor possible to return to the status quo ante in Lebanon, but neither is it desirable or possible to sustain the status quo in the West Bank. And events in Lebanon should enable us to overcome the existing fragmentation of our policy and to relate in a comprehensive approach the three great issues of the Middle East: the Lebanese crisis, the autonomy talks regarding the West Bank and Gaza, and the threat to Western interests in the Gulf.

One of the principal casualties of the Lebanese crises has been the Western illusion — especially prevalent in Europe but rife too in the middle levels of our government, in all recent administrations — that the key to Middle East peace is to be found in a PLO–Israeli negotiation based on various formulas to "moderate" the PLO. It was always a mirage. The colossal effort needed to induce Israel to accept the PLO as a negotiating partner would have forced us to expend all our capital on procedures before substance was reached — even on the highly dubious assumption that it was achievable at all. Nor was it desirable. It would have given a veto on negotiations to the most intransigent element in the Arab world, the group most hostile to the peace process and most closely associated with Arab radicalism with least incentive for restraint. Nor is the PLO a suitable instrument to stabilize the Arab world. It is now clear that Arab support for the PLO has been largely verbal and inspired more by fear of the PLO's capacity for terror than by commitment to its preeminence. No Arab government gave more than verbal support to the embattled Palestinians, and even that lacked the traditional passion. Even Syria stood by passively until its own forces were directly attacked, and made a separate cease-fire while the PLO was being systematically destroyed. When the PLO desperately needed a cease-fire, it turned for help to moderate Egypt, whose peace process it had vilified and at the death of whose leader Palestinians had danced in the street.

American policymakers have reason to be concerned about the

- As part of an interim agreement, special arrangements should be made for the Arab holy places in the old city of Jerusalem.
- Such a goal can be achieved only if the United States spells out what it understands by autonomy in an interim agreement.
- Just as Egypt can be the key Arab country with respect to Lebanon, so must Jordan take the lead on West Bank negotiations.

So far King Hussein has stood aside, conscious of his vulnerability, reluctant to bear the brunt of fighting the PLO and of resisting Syrian pressures, frankly dubious of American understanding of the issues or our resolve to deal with them. But he is much too wise to wish for a PLO state on the West Bank whose initial objective must be his overthrow. And he is much too shrewd not to recognize that the PLO defeat in Lebanon and the demonstration of the limits of Syrian willingness to run risks have given him a window of perhaps two years to take charge of his future. And since Egypt needs Jordanian goodwill in Lebanon just as Jordan requires Egyptian support on the West Bank, there exist the makings of a de facto coalition of moderate Arab states — provided America leads with decisiveness and imagination. The peace process in the Middle East can thus be given a new impetus, especially as events in the Gulf create incentives for Saudi Arabia at least to tolerate and perhaps tacitly to support it.

THE CRISIS IN THE GULF

The governments of the Gulf face a fourfold threat: Shiite radicalism, Moslem fundamentalism, Iranian revolutionary agitation, Soviet imperialism. The last has been the principal focus of American policy although it is far from the most immediate priority of the countries in the area. To them the long-term danger from the Soviet Union pales before the immediate danger from the Iranian revolution. The Soviet Union is relatively far away and is in any case considered a problem only America can solve. Against a backdrop of the consciousness of their own impotence, the countries of the Arabian peninsula are likely

to construe American pleas for assistance against Soviet expansionism as a sign of our weakness. But Iran is close and in its various in-
carnations fulfills all immediate Arab nightmares.

The focus of Iranian pressure at this moment is Iraq. There are
few governments in the world less deserving of our support and less
capable of using it. Had Iraq won the war, the fear in the Gulf and the
threat to our interest would be scarcely less than it is today. Still,
given the importance of a balance of power in the area, it is in our interests to promote a cease-fire in that conflict; though not at a cost
that will preclude an eventual rapprochement with Iran either if a
more moderate regime replaces Khomeini's or if the present rulers
wake up to the geopolitical reality that the historic threat to Iran's independence has always come from the country with which it shares a
border of 1,500 miles: the Soviet Union. A rapprochement with Iran,
of course, must await at a minimum Iran's abandonment of hege-
monic aspirations in the Gulf. There exists at least an opportunity for
a strategic consensus of limited objectives between the United States
and Saudi Arabia and other Gulf states. It must have as its principal
components an American guarantee of the territorial integrity of the
Kingdom and maximum support for its current domestic institutions.
The Arabian peninsula is not the place to exercise our penchant for
experiments with transforming other societies: the structures are too
fragile, our understanding of the historical context and of what is attainable too fragmentary. Nor should this diplomatic effort be dramatic or even public. It must be based in the realization that the
Kingdom is supple as well as subtle, that we do it no favor to interject
it into the forefront of every controversy, exposing it to the pressures
of all contending factions.

But an American policy based on the independence of Lebanon,
fulfillment of attainable Arab aspirations on the West Bank, and protection of the balance of power and institutions in the Arabian peninsula would reconcile all our objectives with those of all our friends in
the area, Arab as well as Israeli.

It would be the best bulwark against Arab radicalism and Soviet
interference. It will require a strong American hand. But as Bismarck
once said, in foreign policy courage and success do not merely stand
in a causal relationship: they are identical.

AMERICAN GLOBAL CONCERNS AND AFRICA

*Extracts from an address before the Second
International Outlook Conference of the South
African Institute of International Affairs, Pretoria,
September 6, 1982*

I AM HONORED by the opportunity to address this distinguished group, in a country whose future evolution is of great, perhaps decisive importance for the prospects of the entire continent, if not of world politics.

And it is, as well, a daunting assignment. For South Africa is geographically almost as far from America as it is possible to be on this globe. Its problems reflect a different history and its domestic structure a contrasting set of values regarding the problem of race. At the same time South Africa has many ties to the industrialized countries and its strategic importance to the free world is undisputed. Thus America's attitude to your country is inevitably ambivalent — a constant tug of war between geopolitical and moral considerations. As I shall point out later, it is in the interest of freedom everywhere that this gap be progressively narrowed and ultimately eliminated.

My assignment here is to describe the international situation as it appears from an American perspective. It must be remembered that from the vantage point of the United States, Africa and southern Africa are part of a larger picture of global concerns, and our attitude toward this continent is incomprehensible otherwise. I will try to trace some of those broad perspectives: the American foreign policy in general; East-West relations; America and Western Europe; and the problems of the developing world. Only in this context can one speak meaningfully about how America regards southern Africa and this country.

THE AMERICAN PERSPECTIVE

The American perspective on world events has undergone dramatic changes in the last generation.

Americans do not have a long experience with foreign affairs. Our founding fathers were quite sophisticated in manipulating the European balance of power to secure our independence. Since then, however, a century and a half of isolation encouraged the illusion in America that we did not really need a foreign policy — or rather, that foreign involvement was purely a matter of choice for us; we could involve ourselves, or not, as we preferred. It took two world wars in this century to shatter this illusion, but certain preconceptions lingered in the American psyche for some decades afterward.

Americans in the isolationist period tended to look down on what they considered the sordid power politics of Europe. Our avoidance of involvement in the balance of power appeared to us not as a boon conferred by distance and the protection of the British Navy, but as a virtue, as a sign of our moral superiority. Since 1945, we have been permanently active in world affairs and have reluctantly had to face the realities of power. Nevertheless, we still tend to view the world in moral terms and to hold ourselves — and our friends — to a high standard of moral conduct as we see it. We fall short of it from time to time but only at heavy cost: the sacrifice of the domestic support needed to sustain American leadership in the world.

For a time after 1945, it seemed relatively easy for us to equate power and morality — the secret American dream. In the aftermath of the Second World War, the United States produced the amazing amount of over half of all the goods and services in the world. We were so overwhelmingly powerful that our allies tended to follow our prescriptions; since we offered them military protection and substantial economic aid, it was a relatively harmonious partnership. The principal developing countries looked to us as the source of capital for their economic development. All this gave Americans a distorted picture of what foreign policy was about; it caused us to identify a fortunate and temporary concatenation with a permanent state of affairs.

The Marshall Plan was in effect a projection of our domestic experience — an overseas application of the New Deal, in which economic progress brought with it political stability almost automatically. And the security problem represented by the Soviet Union, which prompted the Truman Doctrine and the foundation of NATO, seemed analogous to the threat posed by Hitler — that of unambiguous aggression by organized units across recognized frontiers.

It was a creative and brilliantly successful period of American foreign policy, yet never to be repeated. For our world leadership then was grounded in an inherently ephemeral set of conditions.

Since then we have seen that economic progress does not automatically produce political stability — sometimes quite the opposite. And threats to security can be much more manifold than attacks across national borders. Above all, from the late 1960s, for the first time, the United States found itself in the position of having to conduct a foreign policy the way most other nations in history have: as one country among many, unable either to dominate the world or escape from it; forced to seek by persuasion, accommodation, negotiation what it could no longer achieve by unilateral fiat; obliged to learn the traditional techniques of balancing incentives and penalties; required to be steady, reliable, sensitive to marginal shifts in the balance of power and aware of the interconnections between events. Today political, economic, and military power are much more widely diffused and the United States represents only about 21 percent of world GNP — powerful but no longer dominant.

The very balance of power which we have deplored through most of our national experience must henceforth be one of the guiding principles of our foreign policy. Our position toward the rest of the world has become analogous to that of Britain toward Europe for the better part of three centuries. Britain could not permit Europe to be dominated by any single power regardless of its peaceful professions. Britain knew that its resources could not match those of the entire continent; therefore a Europe united against it would sooner or later be able to impose its will. America's global position is no different. If most of the rest of the world fell under hostile control — directly or indirectly — we would be outmatched. Maintaining the balance of power is not a favor we do others but an imperative of our survival.

This confronts us with three major difficulties. Despite the claims of its detractors, America is, as I pointed out, reluctant to base its claims on its power, preferring to prevail by the purity of its maxims. Americans also are uneasy with — indeed, they resent — relative answers, which are the essence of a policy of equilibrium. Throughout our history every problem we have recognized as such proved soluble — that is to say, we found a final answer — if only to overwhelm it with resources. A world in which part of our task is maintaining the balance of power is by definition relativistic, inconclusive, morally unsatisfying.

Therefore, it is no accident that the main lines of the foreign policy that the United States has conducted for most of the postwar period have been attacked consistently by both ends of the political spectrum on the ground that it did not live up to American ideals and offered no final answers — by liberals because it was not sufficiently conciliatory, by conservatives because it was not adequately principled. One extreme tends to view foreign policy as a branch of psychiatry; the basic requirement of diplomacy, in this view, is to generate goodwill. Adversaries are believed to be hostile because they fear or resent us, because we have failed to reassure them that our objectives can be harmonized with theirs. Conflicts are seen to be an aberration from an otherwise natural state of harmony. This school of thought emphasizes unilateral gestures of conciliation; it seeks negotiations regardless of Soviet acts of intransigence — and sometimes especially then. Communists in their view share some similar objectives; Third World nations — no matter how radical their professions — will rally to our standard if we only cleanse ourselves of our past errors.

The opposing school of thought tends to treat foreign policy as a branch of theology. Communism is consummate evil; there is no compromise with the devil. The new nations are either adversaries or cowards. In this view negotiation with the Soviet Union only confuses the American public and is itself a form of moral disarmament. And the new nations should be treated with indifference until they rally to our

side. What is needed is to sound the trumpet, confront our enemies — and the walls of Jericho presumably will crumble.

Both these strains in American thinking, of course, share some
features in common. Neither is comfortable with the notion of a long-
term struggle without a final resolution; with a world in which ideals
can be realized, at any point in time, only imperfectly and always
gradually. Americans are, in some sense, in a state of permanent rebellion against the contemporary realities of world affairs.

Secondly, these psychological difficulties are compounded by
the inherent complexity of assessing the balance of power in the modern period. Historically, military, economic, and political power were
roughly congruent. In our time this is no longer necessarily the case.
Some countries are strong militarily but stagnant politically, for example, the Soviet Union. Some countries, such as several oil-producing states, are powerful economically but weak militarily. Some Third
World nations have at times had a political influence out of proportion
to their military and economic strength: India in the fifties and early
sixties is a good example.

And the time scale for redressing the various balances is not
identical. Restoration of the military balance is occurring more rapidly than the economic or political one. But success in one category of
power does not guarantee success in others.

These tensions produce a third obstacle to a consistent American diplomacy: our tendency to decide foreign policy issues by analogy to domestic disputes. This causes problems to be segmented into
a series of individual decisions resolved by compromises between ad-
versarial positions. In domestic legislation, where each issue is essentially discrete and completed with the passage of a law, this has
proved quite effective — especially as, in the democratic political
tradition, the loser accepts his setback with grace (also with the
knowledge that he has a chance to renew the battle and perhaps prevail on another occasion). But foreign policy is a seamless web. Compromise between philosophical positions may yield the least common
denominator, not the best conceived outcome in terms of a coherent,
consistent long-term national strategy. The continual renewal of our
domestic debate produces the lack of continuity about which some of

our allies especially have complained. Each new administration seems to pride itself on repudiating the methods and assumptions of its predecessor. Leaving aside the merits, such a practice makes for no little uncertainty on the part of other nations. It causes friendly nations which depend on us to hedge their bets; it leaves adversaries confused.

For America, Vietnam was the catharsis that taught us our limits; but reality would have imposed itself in any event. The trauma of having to come to grips with a world of incomplete solutions and relative power is the mark of the American foreign policy debate in the seventies. And we are emerging from it considerably wiser. The reflexive aversion to the balance of power has given way to a recognition of its essentiality. The period of self-doubt has come to an end. While tactical oscillations continue, the main trend of the current foreign policy has wide support.

But our friends must never forget the dual strains of American policy and the powerful impact of our historical convictions. Whatever the importance of geopolitics and equilibrium, however salient they may become in American foreign policy deliberations, the moral dimension of our national tradition will never disappear. At some point our foreign policy will always return to the wellspring of America's aspiration to promote justice, human dignity, and equality. And it will always give these terms a universal cast — not confined to a particular people. The task of American statesmanship is to combine these two strands into a consistent, coherent, and effective foreign policy.

US–SOVIET RELATIONS

With this as a background, let me turn to the East-West conflict. The Soviet Union presents us with a multifaceted challenge: a superpower militarily, stagnant politically, in a crisis economically. The Soviet Union is clearly militarily extremely powerful. Even as the moral claims of its ideology prove more and more hollow, the Soviet system is growing in military strength and geopolitical reach. Historically, the emergence of a new power usually produced a coalition against it, and a new equilibrium could be achieved only after a test of strength. In the nuclear age, such a war would threaten global cataclysm.

The maintenance of peace is therefore a task of unprecedented complexity. It is obviously the duty of the West to maintain the military balance and to resist Soviet expansionism. The Soviet Union *must* learn — through the West's vigilant resistance — that encroachments on the global equilibrium will not be tolerated. It cannot be beyond the West's capability — superior as we are in economic strength — to accomplish this.

However, a great change has taken place in the nature of military power. Strategic nuclear power is no assurance that challenges will be deterred, or countered, locally. In the fifties the industrial democracies relied on their strategic nuclear arsenal, substituting technology for the burden of conventional armament. But the American nuclear superiority began to disappear in the sixties. Technology tended toward equality, and numbers approached levels beyond which additional increments of destructiveness lost all relationship to the objectives likely to be in dispute. Arms control theory and practice, with their formal emphasis on equality, accelerated and legitimized this trend.

Logically, once the Soviet Union acquired the capacity to threaten the United States with direct nuclear retaliation, the American pledge to launch an all-out nuclear war on behalf of Europe was bound increasingly to lose its credibility and public acceptance — and so would NATO's defense strategy. For that strategy now rested on the threat to initiate mutual suicide. But governments were reluctant to face the financial and domestic implications of the conventional force buildup that was required. They continued the existing strategy, seeking to compensate for the implausibility of the pledge of all-out nuclear defense by more emphatic reiteration of it.

The legacy we are left with is a precarious combination of a reliance on nuclear defense, trends toward nuclear stalemate, growing nuclear pacifism, and continued deficiencies in conventional forces. If the democracies are reluctant to resort to nuclear weapons, and if they continue to evade the necessity of building up their conventional forces, then the Western Alliance is left with no defense policy at all, and we are risking the collapse of the military balance that has made possible thirty-five years of Western security, prosperity, and democracy. We will in effect have disarmed ourselves unilaterally while sitting on the most destructive stockpile of weapons that the world has seen.

In these circumstances, the West faces a profound moral as well as practical challenge. The risks of nuclear war produce a feeling of revulsion verging on abdication. Yet if, in the democracies, avoidance of war becomes the sole objective of foreign policy, the world is open to the domination of the most ruthless. The deepest challenge to the democracies is to build support for the proposition that peace must be based on freedom as well as restraint; that leaving the world to the totalitarians can produce horrors even greater than the risks of resistance: witness Indochina.

Thus the West, while maintaining the balance of power, must not lose sight of the moral and political framework that gives it meaning. It is clear that public sentiment in the democratic nations will not sustain a policy of equilibrium without a parallel effort to end or reduce conflict. Electorates will not support defense programs or a vigorous foreign policy if they imagine that their governments are the cause of tensions or if serious efforts are not being made to push back the specter of nuclear war.

It is for this reason that arms control and efforts to reduce tensions have been on the agenda of US–Soviet relations for most of the last fifteen years. Arms control is not a substitute for a secure military balance, but it can be a way of maintaining it at lower levels of forces or of reducing the risks of the outbreak of nuclear conflict by miscalculation or panic. President Reagan has made forthcoming proposals for strategic arms reductions. He has wisely focused not only on reducing the numbers of nuclear weapons, but on those types and characteristics of strategic weapons that most pose the danger of surprise attack or first strike. And he has stressed as well the need for restraint in superpower conduct.

Thus a long-term strategy for dealing with the Soviet Union

must combine power and diplomacy; both resistance to challenges and a willingness to resolve political problems through negotiation; both defense of Western values and a recognition that we are forced to coexist on this planet in an era of thermonuclear weapons.

This becomes all the more important, because the inherent instabilities of the Soviet system will make negotiations inevitable sooner or later.

Both sides in the East-West confrontation are betting on history. And one of the ironies of the postwar period is the extraordinary structural weakness that is now seen to lie beneath the impressive surface of Soviet power.

The Soviet economy is a vast, cumbersome machine burdened with administrative bottlenecks, pervasive inefficiency, and a level of performance that tends toward stagnation. It seems to require a black market, that is, a secret free market, to function at all. The dilemma of Communism is that it seems impossible to run a modern economy by a system of total planning; yet it may not be possible to maintain a Communist state *without* a system of total planning.

In the sixty-five-year history of the Soviet state, it has never managed a legitimate, regular succession of political leadership. The system has failed to deal seriously with the aspirations of the intellectual and managerial elite that industrialization inevitably spawns; instead, the Soviet intelligentsia is a cynical, careerist "New Class" corrupted by privilege, its creativity stifled by heavy-handed political rigidity. And the system has yet to cope with the looming reality of its growing non-Russian population, soon to be a majority, with the severe social and political tensions this will entail.

Finally, in every Communist state — it is almost an historic joke — the ultimate systemic crisis, latent if not evident, is over the role of the Communist party. What is the function of a Communist party once it is entrenched in power? It is not needed to run the government, or the economy, or the military. It is the guardian of an ideological legitimacy that has long since lost its motivating appeal. The party's functionaries specialize in dealing with internal crises which their centralized system has created and external crises into which their ambitions tempt them. In Poland, the Communist party was nearly swept away because of its irrelevance, impotence, and total repudiation by the Polish workers in whose name it claimed to rule. It is another historic joke that the only spontaneous revolutions in industrialized countries have been against *Communist* governments.

And we are only at the beginning of that process of transformation. If Moscow is prevented by a firm Western policy from deflecting its internal tensions into international crises, it is likely to find only disillusionment in the boast that history is on its side.

Then the time for serious negotiations on a broad front will have arrived. The industrial democracies must convey now that they stand ready to negotiate seriously, and that they will respect the legitimate security interests of a Soviet Union conducting the policies of a national state and not of a revolutionary power seeking to overthrow or subvert the existing order. But diplomacy toward the Soviet Union is at the core of some current disputes between the United States and its European allies.

*   *   *

THE DEVELOPING NATIONS: AFRICA

These issues may or may not seem of direct interest to South Africa, but they define the context of American views of Africa and of your own country. And the American perspective of Africa is part of an overall perception of the developing world.

The emergence of the developing countries no doubt will one day be seen as one of the seminal events in world history. In 1945 there were some fifty sovereign states; after a generation of decolonization the number had tripled. Never before had foreign policy to be conducted with such a multiplicity of states in a world of instantaneous communication, shadowed by the specter of nuclear war and under the pressures of a complex economic interdependence. For while the developing nations could not hope to achieve their aims without the aid of the industrialized states, the latter in turn could not sustain their prosperity without an assured supply of energy and raw materials at a fair price.

Mutual need did not necessarily — or at least immediately — produce mutual understanding or even serious dialogue. A vast philosophical gap separated the two sides. Many in the West saw in the new nations a replica of their own constitutional evolution; on the contrary, the new states were quite often in active rebellion against not only the tutelage but the institutions of the colonial powers. There was the naive Western assumption that the challenge to political stability was largely economic; that economic growth would more or less automatically produce political stability. In fact, in many countries, economic development undermined the traditional elements of political order. Iran is a good example. The Shah — for many years hailed as a modernizing secular reformer — was overthrown by a coalition of forces that felt threatened by social progress, led by reactionary feudal landlords who resisted land reform, by mullahs who objected to mass education, women's rights, and the cultural influences of the modern world, and by professionals threatened by the inflation inseparable from industrialization. And the same process could repeat itself elsewhere, under conditions of the success of economic and social advance. The corollary is, of course, that economic and social advance not buttressed by corresponding political change makes an explosion inevitable.

Many new nations, after an initial flirtation with parliamentary democracy, chose some version of Marxism as their model. They did so, ironically, not because of the efficacy of Marxist economics but rather because its political theory provided a kind of answer to the riddle of political legitimacy. Marxism furnished a justification for oligarchic and occasionally one-man rule without the inconvenience of elections. But it brought with it as well the usual baggage of Marxist economic planning with the well-known consequences of stagnation, administrative rigidity, and corruption.

For a while, these Marxist regimes sought to use the so-called nonaligned movement to exact by political pressure the economic development assistance that their system wasted and their politics made meaningless. The secretariat of the so-called Group of 77 fell more or less into their hands. I once reviewed the declarations of the nonaligned conferences in the late 1970s and I found not a single statement of approbation for anything done by the United States nor any criticism of actions by the Soviet Union. Now it is statistically impossible for the United States to be wrong 100 percent of the time and for the Soviet Union never to make a mistake. And it is absurd for a group to call itself "nonaligned" while professing such one-sided views.

Something deeper, more intangible was involved. There existed, to be sure, a certain ideological affinity for "socialism" which came to be identified with the Soviet Union and an understandable resentment of historical colonialism. More important was the consciousness that criticism of the United States involved next to no risk while the penalties for opposition to the Soviet Union could be severe. This was all the more true because many developing countries, and almost all of those of Africa, faced exactly the opposite of the problem of their Western counterparts at a comparable stage of historical evolution. Most Western countries were nations before they formed states; in Africa and elsewhere in the developing world, the state often preceded the nation. Boundaries were frequently artificial, reflecting the convenience and territorial compromises of former colonial rulers. In these circumstances the concept of a loyal opposition — the essence of modern democracy — is difficult to implement. For reality supports the natural temptation of political leaders to consider an assault on their personal position as a threat to domestic cohesion. By the same token, an outside power known to have a considerable capacity for subversion can gain a disproportionate influence.

And yet sooner or later reality will impose itself. The Soviet Union can threaten subversion but offer no useful development program. It exports weapons and proxy troops but no hope for economic or diplomatic progress. Developing countries have learned to rely on it for neither. The nonaligned movement may at last begin to live up to its name. We are thus in a position to think of a serious and realistic economic and political dialogue with the developing nations of Africa and elsewhere based on true reciprocity and without ideological blinders.

The following principles should govern this dialogue:

As a superpower the United States has an interest — together where possible with its allies — to prevent the Soviet Union from exploiting the uncertainties, dislocations, and occasional turmoil of the process of development. Americans are beginning to learn that the danger of subversion or of exploited local discontent must be dealt with in a time frame more immediate than even the best designed process of development and reform. We know that once Soviet totalitarianism — or its various proxy forms — is established, the process is very difficult to reverse. Indeed, under the Brezhnev doctrine the Soviet Union claims the right to impose this irreversibility by force. For all these reasons the United States will not abdicate its strategic interests even when it is less than satisfied with all local circumstances. We will not fail to respond if the Soviet Union or its proxies seek to dominate areas of vital concern to us.

At the same time the developing world, and Africa especially, should not be viewed simply or even primarily as an arena of superpower confrontation. For the objective of our foreign policy must be to create an international system that most of its members wish to maintain. No international order can survive unless the more than one hundred new and developing nations become supporting participants in it. And they will feel that only if they have a stake by sharing in the fruits of progress. The true challenge to the West is not to our economic capacity, but to our political understanding. We should not let ourselves be blackmailed; but we cannot make our contribution to international peace unless we help fulfill the hopes and aspirations of the responsible African states and other members of the developing world. In a broad sense, this is an important component of America's strategic interest in a stable and peaceful international order.

The conditions for such a dialogue have improved considerably in recent years. Developing countries, especially in Africa, need not listen to Western preachments about the hopelessness of the Marxist system; all they have to do is survey the results of African experiments with it. In case after case, socialist models have brought near-bankruptcy to countries richly endowed with natural and human resources and vast potential. This need not continue to be so, but to reverse the trend toward stagnation and decay will require a new look at reality.

It is also becoming clear that tactics of confrontation are self-defeating. Developing nations in Africa are increasingly learning that if they rely on Soviet or proxy forces they will mortgage their independence. And more and more members of the so-called nonaligned grouping are coming to the realization that they must find some relationship between their political rhetoric and their economic and social aspirations. They are sovereign states; they have a right to whatever domestic system and foreign policy they choose. But the industrial democracies are also sovereign, and have a right to give assistance to friends rather than congenital opponents. We have political, economic, and moral reasons to give aid, but Third World nations cannot expect both to conduct foreign policies consistently hostile to us and at the same time to receive our economic support. They will have to decide.

Finally, in a period of austerity in the industrialized world, official aid budgets are not going to be substantially increased. Developing countries will have to adjust to the reality that foreign private investment is the most promising source of development capital. And they will have to reflect about the political and economic incentives to attract such capital.

As for the United States, there is every reason to hope that we have transcended our traditional oscillation between considering the developing nations simply as cold-war pawns and the sentimentality of seeking to win over radicals by pretending to share their slogans. Revolutionaries will not be charmed out of the convictions of a lifetime by invocations of abstract goodwill. The United States is at last prepared for a mature partnership based on mutually realistic expectations. We must find the means both to help the developing countries toward sustainable economic growth and to expand the world trading system which is the key to the well-being of all societies. On this basis there is an unusual opportunity for a new constructive relationship.

SOUTH AFRICA

And so I come at last to my host country, the Republic of South Africa. I am not here with a blueprint of how to solve problems that the centuries have spawned and decades have made intractable. I want to describe how your country's international situation appears to a well-disposed outsider. There seem to me to be four fundamental realities.

First: In terms of resources and technical skill, South Africa is in a unique position to promote the peace and progress of the continent. There would be extraordinary prospects were South Africa able to achieve an accommodation with its neighbors.

Second: Black Africa has an immense stake in the shared enterprise of building security and prosperity in Africa; the potential value of constructive relations with its neighbor to the south should be clear. Black Africa pays an enormous price, moreover, when its countries allow themselves to be occupied by tens of thousands of non-African combat troops — irrespective of the pretext for their being there. There is no profit for Africans if the continent remains a battleground for superpower contention in its crudest form. Those in Moscow and Havana who seek to perpetuate the presence of foreign troops in Africa do not have Africa's interests in mind; they undoubtedly prefer the perpetuation of tensions and seek to *prevent* conditions of cooperation and mutual security among the nations of the continent.

All African states need to face up to this truth. A better alternative is available.

Third: South Africa is of the greatest strategic importance to the non-Communist world, not only geographically but in terms of resources, some of them nearly irreplaceable elsewhere.

Fourth: However, this last reality has one powerful limiting condition. Even the best-disposed Americans are shaped and bound by their country's deeply held ideals of liberty. South Africans must not deceive themselves with comforting thoughts about strategic geography and resources into believing that severe moral and political differences will not override them. Nor can even the most geopolitically oriented American statesmen fail to take into account the aspirations and convictions of the preponderant majority of this continent, as they have been impressed upon me in recent days in Zambia and Zimbabwe.

South Africans have a right to ask for some patience with respect to the special complexities of their situation. But that time is not

'. Those who wish South Africa well, and would like it to take
ce in international affairs, will not be able to find common
und with you as long as the system of institutionalized racial discrimination persists.

The steps that have been taken to ease petty apartheid, the measures to broaden the political rights of coloureds and Indians and the economic conditions of blacks — and the signs that your government is trying to think creatively and promote change (and paying a political price for it) — these are noted, and appreciated. But your friends would render you no service if they implied that these were anything but the first steps on a long journey.

The present policy will *not* provide the ultimate solution to the problem of power sharing, either in political arrangements or homeland policy. Devising a more equitable form of federalism or confederalism — or some other just political institutions — depends on the creativity and determination of *all* the peoples of South Africa. I can only say that a system which respects human dignity, extends due process, provides for equal individual rights, and protects the principle of citizenship will garner sympathetic outside support in many quarters.

The efforts being made to improve the economic and educational status of blacks, moreover, imply their own political logic. As the black population rises in its skills and capabilities, it will increasingly develop its own articulate leadership and consciousness of its condition — and its potential. Thus, as so often before in history, the more genuine the material progress being made by the black community, the more it creates the need for an appropriate political framework.

I do not pretend to know the details of the final destination. Too many outsiders have offered facile slogans drawn from the experience of homogeneous societies and different historical circumstances. Clearly South Africa will have to find its own path. South Africa's friends would eagerly extend support to any constructive solution that embodies the fundamental principles of human dignity, civil rights, and full political participation. The best advice an outsider can offer now is to urge a heroic effort to take the initiative in consultation with all the peoples of this country, to devise new structures and concepts compatible with the fundamental values of other Western societies. History is kind to political leaders who use a margin of choice while it is still available; those who wait on events are usually overwhelmed by them.

The period before pressures become overwhelming should be used for an act of constructive statesmanship. The best way to keep Soviet influence out of the region is first to ameliorate and then to eliminate the conditions which facilitate its entry.

*   *   *

I do not know whether southern Africa is heading for further tragedy, or for a future of progress and reconciliation. I know only that the history of the remainder of this century will be full of dramatic events, and much of the history of that period will be made on this continent. Your beautiful and dramatic country will be a major actor in the unfolding drama. Your friends can only wish you well in any efforts to provide that the continent on which you live can be a showplace for the peace of the world and the reconciliation of the races.

CHALLENGES TO THE WEST IN THE 1980s

*Extemporaneous remarks to the Fifth CSIS
Quadrangular Conference
(Center for Strategic and International Studies),
Georgetown University, Washington, D.C.,
September 20, 1982*

LET ME BEGIN with a quick survey of a number of challenges which I see before us in the 1980s.

Let me introduce it with a saying that our Chinese friends used to use with us when we started calling on them in the early 1970s. The saying was: "There is turmoil under the heavens, but the situation is excellent."

I must admit that on many visits to China the meaning of that remark eluded me, but since I didn't want to admit that there were limits to my capacity to comprehend, I nodded sagely.

The fact is that I would describe the present situation, as far as the United States is concerned, in somewhat similar terms. I think there is turmoil under the heavens, but if one looks at the underlying factors, the situation if not excellent is malleable. We are in one of the periods in which creative policy can make major progress and in which, in almost any area of policy we consider, the possibilities of new departures for creative action seem very considerable indeed.

AMERICA'S ADJUSTMENT

In fact, one of the biggest problems we have is psychological or philosophical. It is that the 1980s are a period in which the United States has to conduct foreign policy as other nations have had to conduct foreign policy throughout their history. In the 1950s the United States represented some 52 percent of the world's Gross National Product. Under those circumstances, our foreign policy was really a problem of identifying issues and overwhelming them with resources.

Our allies were largely dependent on us and our adversaries needed primarily to be convinced that we meant business on whatever issue concerned us most. Every decade since then, the percentage of the world's total Gross National Product which the United States represents has declined by some 10 percent. Now the United States represents some 21 or 22 percent of the world's Gross National Product. It still makes us the single largest economic unit, but it imposes on us necessities against which our historical tradition has rebelled.

We now, for the first time in our history, face a situation in which if the whole rest of the world were to fall under hostile domination we would be clearly outmatched. Our policy from now on must be more like that pursued by Britain toward the continent of Europe through several centuries. It was a principle of British policy that a Europe united under the rule of a single dominant power would be in a position to outmatch and endanger Great Britain; therefore, Britain made itself the balancer of the European equilibrium, a role it fulfilled by acting soberly, rather unemotionally, based on a careful assessment of the balance of power.

With respect to the rest of the world, the United States is today in an analogous position. Maintaining the equilibrium is no longer a favor we do for other nations. It is an imperative of our survival. The balance of power, decried as it is in our international relations textbooks, is not the end of our foreign policy but it has to be the beginning of our foreign policy. Its requirements have to be studied over an extended period of time, and what is more, have to be carried out over an extended period of time.

It is characteristically American that every new administration begins convinced not only that it will change the world, but that it created the world. Sooner or later, that process has to stop. Sooner or later, a consensus has to develop, not on every tactical move we make on individual issues, but on the fundamental requirements of our national interest — reluctant as we are to think in terms of national interest.

There are many here who have heard me say it before, but the debate which we Americans tend to carry on is still too much couched in categories that imply that there are final answers, that there is a final goal toward which we are working, called peace, after which tensions presumably disappear. There is too much of a division in our national debate between the psychiatric school of foreign policy, which thinks relations among nations are like relations among people and which emphasizes unilateral concessions and gestures of almost personal goodwill, and the theological school of foreign policy, which implies that the only reason the walls of Jericho have not tumbled yet is because the right ideological trumpet has not yet been sounded.

Our foreign policy henceforth, and that of all industrial democracies, is bound to have to concern itself with an adjustment of relative balances. Our situation is complicated by the fact that many in Europe paradoxically have moved to positions that they used to criticize and regard as peculiarly American in the early postwar period — naive reliance on the strenuous exercise of goodwill to remove objective difficulties with adversaries and insistence that there be conclusive proof of the aggressive intentions of potential opponents before one takes irrevocable or major steps.

With this as a background, let me discuss a number of particular issues. Rather than give you my conclusions with respect to them, let me state either the problems as I see them, or some general principles of action.

THE MIDDLE EAST

As a general proposition, I do not believe that this is the time for me to make basic pronouncements in detail about the Middle East. Fundamentally, I think that all of us concerned with foreign policy should support the Administration through the difficult days and weeks ahead. On the other hand, I would like to state a number of general observations.

I believe that the opportunity to make major progress toward peace in the Middle East has never been greater, despite the tragic and inexcusable events of the last few days in Beirut, and despite the passions that preceded them. The fact has been demonstrated that the Soviet Union is able to supply weapons but no solutions; that the countries of the rejectionist front in the Arab world can define a rhetoric but no program; that, on the other hand, Israel's claim to be seriously threatened must have been strongly mitigated by its military success. And all parties in the area must have learned that a continuation of this cycle of violence cannot possibly serve anybody's interest.

We must take advantage of this opportunity. Let me confine myself today to a number of principles.

First, the issue of the West Bank and Gaza, what the Israelis call Judea and Samaria and the Gaza District, cannot be settled by annexation by Israel. This is not something derived from the Camp David Agreement; this has been a fundamental position of every American administration since 1967. It is in that context that the Administration's opposition to the settlements policy of the Begin government should be considered.

Second, the partner for this negotiation should be the Kingdom of Jordan. But it is important to define what that means, as I will explain further when I discuss US–European relations. It cannot mean that Jordan should provide merely a mantle of legitimacy for a PLO entity that then becomes an incubus within the Jordanian state. It must be genuine Jordanian participation, in which Jordan will assume real responsibilities on the West Bank.

Third, while Israel must not identify its security with the annexation of the West Bank and Gaza, equally its security cannot be defined simply in terms of recognition by its neighbors and normalization of relations with them. Recognition of the existence of participants in a negotiation is the beginning of wisdom in foreign policy. It is what all other nations get for nothing. It is not something which entitles countries or groups to special compensation. In other words, the question of security must be given a concrete content and it is a legitimate subject of negotiation, even if it cannot be pushed to the point of annexation.

Fourth, it is important for Israel and for all other countries to understand that the dignity and self-respect of the Arab nations is an important factor and that proceeding simply by the creation of unilateral faits accomplis is no basis for the conduct of foreign policy and even less for the relations between close allies.

Fifth, it is also important for Israel's allies and other nations, irritated as they may be by acts of unilateralism and insensitivity, not to make confrontation the defining principle of their foreign policy. They must keep in mind that for a nation with a narrow margin of survival, the dividing line between arrogance and panic, between self-assurance and hysteria, can be very narrow. In the face of all provocation I would urge some compassion and understanding and a resumption of dialogue.

This is as far as I will go today, and I think the audience here can see that it is compatible with the main lines of the foreign policy that the Administration is pursuing, even if as it evolves a different content may be given by different people to this or that proposition.

EUROPEAN-AMERICAN RELATIONS

Let me now turn to European-American relations. I will be relatively brief. Some of the difficulties that exist between Europe and the United States — it has been said at great length and repeatedly — are due to the success of previous Western policies: the recovery of Europe, the corresponding growth of a sense of identity, and the inevitable tendency that the continent which developed the concept of sovereignty was never going to find its purpose in sharing our burdens but in developing perceptions of its own.

However one may explain it, there seem to me to be two major problems that must be solved.

First, there is the issue of military strategy. The facts are perfectly clear: The strategy developed in the early 1950s cannot possibly continue into the 1980s. Perpetuating the theory that American strategic nuclear power can protect Europe against all contingencies inevitably will lead to a combination of demoralization, pressures for unilateral disarmament, and a failure to build up conventional forces. The issue has been ducked for fifteen years or hidden behind percentage figures of budgetary increase that never got to the heart of the problem of what strategy is really appropriate for the eighties and nineties. The only possible strategy is one that builds up conventional forces to resist foreseeable challenges. There are no shortcuts, there are no gimmicks. Ideas like renouncing the first use of nuclear weapons will have the inevitable consequence of stigmatizing the weapons on which Alliance defense must still in part depend, or will create the dangerous impression that the West may accept a conventional defeat rather than in the end resort to nuclear retaliation. But the converse is not true. It is not true that we can continue to rely on essentially the strategy of the fifties and sixties, modified with a gimmick here and a new technology there. That is the fundamental problem in strategy, and it underlies the arms control policies that must be related to it.

The second problem has to do with East-West relations. We have now gone through a period of exuberant détente and then through a period in which détente was retrospectively made to carry the blame for all the difficulties that were caused by our domestic divisions on other subjects. It is now time to address the fundamental question of how we should conduct East-West relations over an extended period of time.

We are at a moment when the Soviet Union is in enormous difficulty, when it is foreseeable that sometime in the eighties some Soviet leaders must ask themselves how much longer they can run an economy as unbalanced as the one that they now maintain; they must ask themselves how long they can govern a system that cannot manage a legitimate succession, an economy that is assailed by shortages and surpluses at the same time — a problem that no Communist country has yet solved. At that point, a possibility for serious negotiations must arise — provided that we do not make the mere fact of negotiation an issue in our national debate, with one group considering any conference progress toward a settlement, and another group considering any meeting with Soviet negotiators as a pact with the devil. Our problem is to define what in a serious negotiation we would ask of the Soviets; what we are prepared to pay in return for what we consider restrained international conduct; and, indeed, how we define restrained international conduct on both sides.

Now that requires, however, that we husband our assets. And it implies that we have to avoid unilateral concessions, either the unilateral disarmament that so many so-called peace movements attempt to impose on us or the unilateral concessions in economic relations that in so many countries in Europe are identified with détente.

Fundamentally what the Soviets want from us in economic relations is irreplaceable for them elsewhere: food, technology, general know-how. What they pay in return — if they pay anything in return — is raw materials that are relatively easily replaceable for us. In these circumstances, trade would have long since assumed minimal proportions were it not constantly fueled by concessional prices and concessional credits. It will seem incomprehensible to future generations that the West was not able to develop a coherent East-West economic policy and that it was not able to exact a political quid pro quo for the economic benefits it was unilaterally bestowing on the Soviet Union.

I do not think that the timing and the tactics of the American decision on the [Soviet natural gas] pipeline will go down in history as classic examples of modern diplomacy. I do believe, however, that the questions raised by the President's pipeline decision were important. And I cannot endorse the self-righteous confrontational reaction of so many of our allies who hide behind allegations that they were simply carrying out obligations and make debating points that since we were selling grain they had a right to sell the pipeline. Everybody knows that if we stopped selling grain tomorrow the pipeline would still go forward. The question raised by the Administration was fundamental. Incidentally, I am not a wild supporter of the grain sales, either.

I do not join those who argue that an economic boycott of the Soviet Union can bring about a collapse of the Soviet system. I do believe that the Soviet Union understands best a negotiation on the basis of strict reciprocity. And I think it is a failure of Western leadership that we have not been able to define for ourselves what it is we want from the Soviet Union in the political field or that we have not been able to agree with each other on credit policies and pricing policies that are in the common interest.

The lesson to be drawn from the pipeline affair is not by what face-saving formula we can end the immediate crisis — which clearly, if rationality prevails, will be ended before matters get totally out of control — but rather whether we can use the pipeline crisis to fashion a fundamental agreement among the industrial democracies about how they visualize East-West economic relations and for what political price. The democracies should do so in the context that they are prepared to have these economic relations with the East in order to support a fundamental negotiation — a fundamental negotiation that they are also prepared to define for themselves and that is not driven by the need to placate public pressures on a year-to-year basis. I suspect that if the various arms control proposals are analyzed in detail, we would find that they are much too much driven by the need to deal with immediate pressure groups and much too little geared to the security situation we foresee in the middle eighties. What is true of arms control is even more true of East-West economics.

Let me make a final point about European-American relations. It is not possible, nor is it desirable, that we pursue parallel policies all over the world, but it is also not possible or compatible with the Alliance that we agree on *no* major policy around the world. It seems to me that we are perilously close to drifting into such a state of affairs. In Central America one can only say that several European policies are deliberately designed to, or have the practical consequence of, undercutting what we are attempting to do. I am not saying that we are inevitably right, but I do maintain that when a major country acts in an area it considers of vital importance, its allies owe it some respect for its views, as we attempted to show in the Falkland crisis vis-à-vis Great Britain.

And we see it again in recent weeks with respect to the Middle East. A fundamental objective of the President's speech of September 1 [1982] seems to me to have been the introduction of Jordan into the negotiations. How can that process possibly be helped when PLO leaders are feted all over Europe and their status is enhanced before anybody has seen even the slightest indication of what conclusions they have drawn from their defeat in Lebanon? Why is it so impossible for us and the Europeans at least to discuss our assumptions?

How can it fail to lead to a fundamental rupture, sooner or later, if totally different strategic conceptions are simultaneously pursued?

LATIN AMERICA

Let me make a few observations about Latin America. Of all the areas in the world, the one about which my opening quotation about "turmoil under the heavens" and "an excellent situation" may be least true is Latin America.

We have recently seen in Mexico the impact of economic crisis on the political orientation of a country and the temptation to use foreign opponents as a means of rallying opinion behind authority. And in the aftermath of the Falkland crisis, many Latin American countries are undergoing fundamental reexamination of their orientations: The military, because they feel they can no longer count on the unquestioning support of the United States, resulting in a tendency toward a kind of populism. The radicals, because their relative position has been strengthened. The moderates, because the OAS system is clearly in need of reexamination. And all of them because the international economic structure or, at any rate, the international financial structure, no longer has a fundamental framework for resolving its difficulties.

Few people invite me to speak about economic problems — to their great loss — but they can't keep me from mentioning them once I have a rostrum. If we continue to treat foreign debt by analogy to domestic debt, this is going to prevent any serious examination of issues that are at least political. The theory that foreign governments can be made creditworthy by austerity measures the way domestic debtors can be made creditworthy by self-discipline misunderstands the nature of many developing societies. In a developed country, IMF conditionality often enables governments to provide an alibi for what they would like to have done anyway. In many developing countries, on the other hand, conditionality based on purely economic criteria may be a cure worse than the disease. It may not be sustainable by the political process and may bring about revolutionary conditions which will magnify all the difficulties that those countries are attempting to solve. Or else it creates a kind of cynicism in which the conditions are accepted and never carried out and then provide a rallying point for extreme nationalism later on.

I have no answer to this problem. I know that it cannot be dealt with by business as usual. I do not say that there should be no conditions, only that they should be related to the political needs of fragile societies. Some kind of new financial structure, something like the Bretton Woods understandings, must emerge. Present policies cannot go on forever without leading, if not to an economic crisis, to an unmanageable loss of political confidence. All of these problems exist more acutely in the Western hemisphere than anyplace else. The Western hemisphere is also the area where American creativity can still make the biggest difference.

CONCLUSION

I could go on to other problems, but I think I have made my fundamental point. It is that inevitably when one speaks before a group like this, one emphasizes difficulties. If you analyze the difficulties I have described, they are all amenable to policy solutions either by the United States or by the industrial democracies taken together. If you analyze the difficulties which other parts of the world face, they require systemic changes. There is no way the Soviet system can solve its problems without some sort of constitutionalism by which leaders can be replaced, if not by democratic means, then by some regular procedure. There is no way their economy can operate efficiently on the basis of total planning. And there is no way many of the developing countries can progress through the mixture of Marxism, Third World radical rhetoric, and inefficient governments that now characterizes them.

We have a rare opportunity for creative leadership. The West has the problem fundamentally of a reluctance to face the facts of power, to develop a calculus of incentives and penalties in dealing with the East. Americans have a national reluctance to face up to the reality of only contingent answers and permanent responsibilities. We are handicapped by a domestic process in which decisions are made by adversary proceedings, which gives a premium to each of the contenders for the President's attention to exaggerate his position and creates the concurrent temptation to settle each dispute by some phraseology that either permits each party to do what he wanted to do in the first place or which represents a sort of waffled consensus. These are real problems, but all of them are problems we should know how to solve, and we, I think, are getting better at it.

AFTER LEBANON: A CONVERSATION

An interview with Dr. Kissinger by the editors of The Economist, *published in* The Economist, *November 13, 1982*

DO YOU *see still, after recent events, an opportunity for progress in the Middle East?*

The circumstances for progress in the Middle East are the best I can remember.

Is the Reagan plan one component in that?

Let me define what I consider to be the essential elements of the Reagan plan: (1) that the negotiating partners on the West Bank should be Jordan and Israel; (2) that the West Bank authority elected by Palestinians should be associated with Jordan; (3) that annexation of the West Bank and Gaza by Israel will not be accepted by the United States or by any other country; (4) that there be a moratorium on new Israeli settlements on the West Bank during a peace process; (5) that the negotiation must deal with Israel's security as well as recognition.

There are other aspects of the plan that I think are not as essential.

Now, suddenly, one is able to talk in these terms whereas, say, a year ago it was difficult to see one's way ahead. Were the military events in Lebanon a useful beginning of this process?

Like it or not, they changed things — so that out of the rubble there came the chance of a fresh beginning. I do not believe it would have been possible to achieve the kind of Arab reaction evoked by the Reagan plan had these military operations not taken place. First of all, Lebanon strengthened the moderates in the Arab world by weakening the radicals. Second, it revealed the hollowness, or the limits, of Soviet support for its clients in the Middle East; the Soviets can supply arms but give no impetus to diplomacy. Third, it exposed the fact

that the new generation of American weapons seems to be much superior to the new generation of Soviet weapons. . . .

American weapons with some Israeli frills . . .

With some Israeli frills, yes, but at any rate making the military option
for those using Soviet weapons in the region less and less promising — and in the process devaluing Russia's principal export.

Finally, the lack of effective support for the PLO by the radical
Arab states made it clear that the rejectionist front had rhetoric but
no program. All this eliminated to a large extent the military potential
of the PLO. Therefore if the Palestinians are to participate in the
peace process, it will have to be as a political and not as a military
factor. These are the new objective conditions on the Arab side making for progress.

On the Israeli side the Lebanese action has removed, substantially, the argument that there was an imminent military threat to the
existence of the Jewish state. It would have been unthinkable a few
months ago that an Israeli prime minister would tell his parliament
that for the first time in Israel's history all its frontiers were secure.

For all those reasons conditions have never been better for negotiations — provided the Reagan plan is seen as a framework and
not a blueprint, every last provision of which needs to be implemented
as part of an agreement.

*Which elements of it do you see, then, as being particularly en-
couraging as a framework?*

Jordan as a negotiating partner; a decisive role, a political role, for the
inhabitants of the West Bank and Gaza in determining their political
future, within the framework of association with Jordan; the recognition of Israeli security concerns on the West Bank; and the clear statement by the United States, which will remove any illusions that may
have existed in Israel, that annexation (overt or disguised) is not an
option we will support.

*Those are the potential strengths in the Reagan plan. What are the
potential weaknesses and dangers in it?*

Some of the language is perhaps necessarily ambiguous; some of it will be interpreted differently by the various parties and — I suspect — by different elements of our bureaucracy. This involves the risk of stalemate in the negotiations, tensions with friends on both sides, and disagreement within our government.

The phraseology on Jerusalem in my view may well be only compatible with turning Jerusalem into a UN [United Nations] city, which is a non-starter. The phraseology that the location of the borders will depend on the degree of normalization that the countries are prepared to undertake meets only part of the problem. It obscures the peculiar difficulty of Arab-Israeli negotiation in which one side has attempted to achieve annexation by subterfuge and the other side tries to evade all its problems by trading its maximum demands in return for recognition. In other words, the location of the West Bank border must be related to security as well as to recognition. Israel — as President Reagan has also implied—should not be asked to find security *solely* in recognition.

You talk of the "peculiar difficulty" of Arab-Israeli negotiations.

Two nostalgic illusions inhibit these negotiations. The Israeli nostalgia is that somehow or other they can maneuver events to a de facto annexation of the West Bank. The Arab nostalgia is that somehow or other, having lost the military option, they can maneuver us into accomplishing their maximum program in return for verbal formulas, in the process demoralizing Israel and with luck bringing about its collapse.

Another danger is that the Reagan plan will turn into a subterfuge for rehabilitating the PLO, establishing it with essentially unchanged composition and program on the West Bank, theatening simultaneously Israel and Jordan.

The final danger is psychological. Having taken the unprecedented step of introducing a plan without consultation with Israel, we have to be careful not to turn an emergency measure into a regular procedure. Opposition to Israel must not become a congenital feature of our foreign policy lest we break Israel's back psychologically. This is not the case now; I am simply warning against turning what was a probably unavoidable first step into a permanent feature of our diplomacy.

Is this argument between America and Israel different in nature from previous arguments?

I think that the crisis in American-Israeli relations that resulted from the Reagan speech is unusual in the sense that, for the first time, a presidential plan was put forward without consultation with the Israelis, and for the first time a presidential proposal was totally rejected. We've had tactical disagreements within an agreed strategy before, but this time the dispute involved a fundamental issue of principle. There probably was no other choice; there was a boil that needed lancing in that the Israeli definition of Palestinian autonomy and the definition that the Americans or the Arabs could give to the term had been at fundamental variance from the beginning.

The Israeli proposal for autonomy foresaw a self-governing authority arising out of some process of election. Because the *arrière-pensée* of at least the key members of the Israeli government was, as is now apparent, that they would not give up sovereignty over any part of the West Bank, they were careful not to draw any territorial distinction. By implication the autonomy plan applied to the entire West Bank within the 1967 borders. Paradoxically, the Begin government, against its preferences and ideology, was really proposing what all other nations were certain to treat as an embryo Palestinian state and, to compound the irony, within the 1967 border since none other was under discussion. Once there was an elected self-governing authority on the West Bank, an irreversible political fact would be created on the territory over which its authority was supposed to run. However limited this authority, it would soon turn into the nucleus of something like a Palestinian state, probably under PLO control. It would be so treated by almost all of the countries of the world except Israel.

And that would be something to avoid, in your book?

Well, it was clearly the main objective of the Israeli government to avoid it; its proposal was incompatible with its strategy. All this led to an inherent misunderstanding between the United States and Israel, not to speak of between Egypt and Israel. The only way the Israeli government could avoid the implications of its own proposal was to deprive the word *autonomy* of its dictionary meaning — for example, by elaborating a distinction between autonomy of persons and autonomy of land. Deadlock between Egypt and Israel and latent tensions between the United States and Israel were thus built into the definitions of the problem.

Not to mention Sadat.

And Sadat. Between Sadat and Israel: it probably contributed to weakening Sadat's position. It also fostered an American illusion that perhaps one could get around the problem by enumerating the powers of the self-governing authority. But the problem was insoluble because Israel was not really thinking of autonomy in any commonly accepted use of the word. Even without Lebanon, a showdown on that issue was inevitable sooner or later — the logical implications of the Israeli plan and the way the Israeli government wanted to implement and negotiate it had grown incompatible.

Are you saying that since Camp David we have got stuck on an escalator, so to speak, on the use of the word autonomy *which we now cannot get off?*

No, I'm saying that so long as some form of Israeli sovereignty over the entire West Bank was the objective the autonomy negotiations could not be brought to a conclusion acceptable to all parties; even without Lebanon a point would have been reached at which either the United States would have had to put forward its own definition of autonomy, or there would have been a blowup of the negotiations.

Lebanon has now made it possible to involve other Arab states in the process and therefore to come up with a more comprehensive approach than would have been possible otherwise. That is the boil the Reagan plan has helped lance.

Because it got back to the idea of Peres and others that Jordan ought to be the negotiating partner?

The idea preceded Peres and should not be identified primarily with internal Israeli politics. It has been American policy since 1967 that Jordan should be the interlocutor for the West Bank.

Now, Jordan is talking with Arafat and the PLO. Does that not pose the danger that, by introducing Jordan into it, all we're doing is introducing the PLO on to the West Bank where it can be a threat either to Israel or to Jordan or to both?

That is the key strategic question we must all be clear about. The Reagan plan must not turn into a device for introducing the PLO in its present form and with its present concepts on the West Bank. Jordan would thereby become not so much the principal negotiating partner as a cover for the PLO domination of the West Bank. By making the PLO part of Jordan it will also lay the basis for the eventual PLO takeover of all of Jordan, reversing the events of 1970. The creation of another radical state with irredentist aims toward both Jordan and Israel is irreconcilable with the stability of the Middle East.

Do you feel that point of view is solidly enough embedded in the Reagan plan and in the thinking behind it?

I suspect it is solidly in the mind of the Secretary of State [George Shultz] and of the President. I am not sure it is equally solidly embedded in the minds of all those who have to execute it. It is clearly contrary to the convictions of our European allies. A strategic decision has to be made whether the proposed negotiations seek to make Jordan the principal negotiating partner or whether they are used as a subterfuge for resurrecting the PLO after its defeat. If we are not clear about this, we will not be clear about whatever else to do. Our European allies, especially, must understand that for them to build up the PLO while we emphasize the role of Hussein is certain to lead to paralysis or worse.

But is the PLO — its military option apparently destroyed, and deserted as it was by its Arab friends when it needed to exercise it — really such a threat now?

That remains to be seen; the future evolution of the PLO is one of the key questions before us. I believe its military option has been substantially destroyed except perhaps for terrorism. I would also think that reasonable Palestinians, reflecting about their experience of the past ten or fifteen years, should come to a Sadat-like insight that they must coexist with Israel in some form: they more than any other people, despite — and perhaps because of — the common suffering Israel and the Palestinians have inflicted on each other. If that happens, a new Palestinian leadership may well emerge, perhaps even under the label of PLO. That would not represent such a threat; it could even turn into a major opportunity. The PLO in its present composition and with its present program cannot make such a claim. If the PLO is now resurrected without fundamental structural and philosophical changes, it is likely to remain radical, seeking to upset the equilibrium on the West Bank and to destabilize moderate governments in the area — starting with Jordan. I think it should be given an opportunity to demonstrate a change of approach. But this requires more than ambiguous phrases hinting at recognition of Israel. It presupposes a true turn toward the political option reflected in the PLO's structure, program, and personalities.

Can Arafat, now that the PLO is dispersed and has its military teeth drawn, carry a suitably reformed organization into association with Jordan?

I do not know and perhaps he does not either.

What specific measures should be negotiated on the West Bank for Israel's security?

There is no such thing as absolute security, but there is such a thing as absolute insecurity. As President Reagan pointed out, the narrow neck of Israel between Haifa and Tel Aviv, with a width of only nine miles in some places, cannot be considered a secure frontier whatever the degree of Arab recognition of Israel. The areas essential for an improvement in Israel's security on the West Bank are not heavily populated by Arabs. Thus it should be possible to return to the overwhelming majority of Arabs living on the West Bank and Gaza a controlling voice in facing their future. The precise location of these security frontiers will have to be settled by negotiation.

Is recognition of Israel a starting point for negotiation or the end result?

In negotiations between Israel and Arabs the question of recognition plays a disproportionate and unprecedented role.

In all other negotiations mutual recognition is assumed at the outset. I know no other negotiation in which a country is asked to accept recognition of its existence as the principal quid pro quo. The Israelis sometimes give the impression that their sole objective is recognition, and some Arabs, perhaps sensing the opportunity, seem to imagine that they can achieve their maximum program in return for nothing more than simple recognition. So I would be much more interested in how the PLO in fact conducts itself toward the peace process than in arcane formulas of recognition. However, the issue of recognition has become so symbolic that it cannot be avoided. Recognition of Israel is the beginning of a process, not the end; it does not meet — by itself — the needs of the situation. It is not, when all is said, much of a concession for the PLO to make. Many recognized states nevertheless wound up being destroyed even in our own time.

It comes down to some extent to Israel's sense of being threatened. You have said that Israel's claim to be threatened has either been eliminated or strongly mitigated after the Lebanon military conflict. Does Israel really have as many reasons as it claims it has to go on being fearful?

In the immediate future, say over five years, it probably has less reason to be militarily fearful than at any time in its history. However, over an historic period a nation of three million, in whatever borders can be conceived, surrounded by a hundred million people that will never be fully reconciled to (even once they have accepted) its existence, has reason to be uneasy. After all, India has recognized Pakistan as a state and yet one would not describe the relations between them as one of great confidence; Pakistan's sense of being threatened has, rightly or wrongly, never abated. It has remained a root fact of Pakistani politics and diplomacy and I suspect it will be a root fact of Israeli politics even after peace has been negotiated.

Second, the rate at which arms now pour into the area from all sides will sooner or later erode Israel's present qualitative superiority.

Finally, Israel must feel, perhaps only subconsciously, that total dependence on a distant superpower is extremely dangerous and precarious. It is, after all, the essence of a superpower that its perceptions of the dangers may not be calculated by yardsticks relevant to a small country. The Israelis may feel, more than they dare articulate, that for a nation with a narrow margin of survival, and a people with a history of catastrophe, the line between arrogance and hysteria, between overweening behavior and panic, is very narrow. If they are pressed too close to that line there could be a political and psychological collapse or a convulsive eruption. This fear is at the same time the secret dream of some of Israel's adversaries.

You drew attention to that thin dividing line when writing about your own negotiations with Israel. Are we not in danger of elevating that concept in Israel, whereas what we ought to be trying to do is diminish it, and to elevate in its place a combination of more realism and more self-confidence, which would allow Israel both to negotiate and to exist?

Well, at this point I don't think Israeli self-confidence needs any particular encouragement. Yes, we should encourage Israel to negotiate. Israel is more likely to do so, paradoxically, if it feels compassion on our side, maybe even affection, rather than unremitting pressure. Where we disagree with Israel on substantive points we must be prepared to express this — strongly if necessary. But it is a very difficult maneuver to bring off — to press Israel on individual points, as we must do with perseverance, and yet not cumulatively to harass it into emotional and psychic collapse.

This is also important in terms of our negotiating position with the Arabs. Arab leaders are given an incentive to be conciliatory only so long as it is clear that our support requires reasonable and moderate positions on their part. If, however, the impression spreads that across-the-board opposition to Israel is built into us, so to speak, then their temptation to stick to their maximum program is very great. In other words, I feel that pressure on Israel should be exerted retail rather than wholesale, if one can put it in such crude terms.

You talk of the conditions for Arabs getting "our support." Yet American support for Israel during the past eighteen months has often been flouted, to the point that the Arabs must wonder what it is worth. Can America afford to see its wishes ignored so openly by a small, determined ally? And what, if it cannot, should it do about it?

The Israeli outrage at the unilateral procedures preceding the Reagan plan would have had more moral force had not Israel proceeded unilaterally on a whole series of issues and had it not made challenging our views, sometimes provocatively, almost a principle of policy. America must, as I have said, treat Israel compassionately and seriously. It must do its serious best to achieve prior agreement before taking initiatives affecting Israel's future. In the end we cannot abdicate the definition of our national interests to a small friendly country, however close. Responsible Israeli leaders will know that continual open challenges to our government, especially to the President, risk the public support for the sustained assistance on which their policy ultimately depends.

No sanctions?

I would hope such a point will never be reached.

It has been an American position and, indeed, almost a universal position since 1967 that the West Bank cannot and should not be annexed by Israel — yet, expressed in terms of concrete, it is being annexed or already has been. Is it now any longer conceivable to talk in terms of negotiation over the West Bank?

It is not only conceivable; it is imperative. Annexation of the West Bank — overt or disguised — will sow the seeds of endless crises, one of which will inevitably erupt into conflagration. It is not even in the interest of Israel however narrowly conceived. The incorporation of Gaza and the West Bank into Israel will sooner or later produce an Arab majority that will destroy the essence of the Jewish state. And if Israel seeks to escape this dilemma by expelling all the Arabs it will lose the moral support of even its best friends. Over an historical period Israel would not be able to withstand the crisis that would result.

Begin has called the idea of an association between Jordan and the West Bank "grotesque." Should he be required, or asked, in a negotiation to change his mind — and what form of pressure can be brought by the United States to help persuade him to change his mind?

This is the fundamental issue between the United States government and Begin, so it is unfair to make him the symbol of negotiating difficulties. With respect to Egypt, after all, he made more concessions than I would have expected on the basis of my experience with previous Israeli governments. Granted all this, the present positions of the American and Israeli governments are nearly irreconcilable. As for pressures in the immediate future, the most effective one is for King Hussein to step forward with whatever Arab acquiescence he needs as the Arab negotiator for the West Bank. This would pose for all Israelis the concrete necessity for decisions. So long as the Arab participation in the process remains only hypothetical, the debate will be sterile and bitter. In the meantime the best that America can do is to state a reasonable definition of what it has in mind with respect to both security and to political evolution. If Hussein steps forward and we stick to our course, many Israeli fears will be reduced and responsible opinion in Israel will shift toward such a program. We need a serious discussion with the Israelis on what we understand to be the security frontiers on the West Bank and what territories we expect would have to be returned.

We need as well a serious dialogue with especially the moderate Arabs. Moderate Arabs must know that their views will be respectfully heard in America; they must not be encouraged to believe that their sole contribution to the negotiations is the willingness to accept Israel. They must avoid the temptation of building an Arab consensus on the prospect of a gradual demoralization of Israel by American pressure. They as well as Israel should work with us on the definitions of peace and security that are central to the peace process.

Should America be proposing these?

As a last resort, yes.

Prior agreement with Israel rather than prior agreement with Hussein?

Hussein will have to be part of the process; indeed, it cannot start without him. Once negotiations begin, Hussein has to know what we are discussing with Israel and has to be given an opportunity to express his views. In a serious, sustained negotiation with Hussein I do not believe that any Israeli government could maintain oppposition in principle to the return of the overwhelming majority of the Arab populations to some form of genuine Arab control. Therefore there should now be a moratorium on further theoretical exegesis of the Reagan plan; the urgent problem is to induce the relevant parties to start negotiating. The Israelis could maintain their position that they are negotiating on the basis of Camp David, and the Arab side would invoke the Reagan plan; the President has after all declared the terms are compatible.

Why should Arafat agree that Hussein step forward?

Because this is the only way the Palestinians can achieve control over their future. The alternative to the course outlined here is not a PLO state but Israeli annexation of the West Bank and the loss of an historic opportunity.

Do you feel able to define, in any negotiating terms, what those genuine forms of Arab control would be? And what the relationship, for example, between Jordan and a West Bank entity of some kind would be?

The Arab population on the West Bank and Gaza must be given a serious opportunity to express their preferences, which means free of Israeli pressure as well as of PLO intimidation. The first phase should be Jordanian control of the West Bank minus agreed Israeli security zones. Jordanian territory on the West Bank would — as seems generally agreed — be demilitarized. Under Jordanian aegis a process to elicit the genuine preferences of the Palestinians should then be started. This can take many forms, some as yet unforeseeable, but maintaining an association with Jordan is central. I do not believe that it is in the interests of the majority of Arab states to create a Libyan or a South Yemenite type of regime on the West Bank.

Unlikely, given the nature of Palestinians, isn't it?

Unlikely unless outside pressures can be exercised in the form of terrorism. As the Palestinians develop an organization that is genuinely geared to a political rather than to a military contest — or adapt existing organizations to that process — we should be openminded with respect to their ultimate role. It would be more appropriately negotiated between the Palestinians and Jordan and other moderate Arab states than by us.

We've talked about the dangers inherent in any form of pressure put on Israel . . .

I am not saying "any" form of pressure. It is the nature of Israel's politics that its leaders probably can make some concessions only when it is absolutely clear that America cannot be persuaded to an alternative; therefore it is imperative for the United States to be ready to state its own view and to persevere in the face of opposition. But it also requires, as I have said, acceptable Arab interlocutors with a reasonable program.

That raises the second question I was coming to about pressure on Israel: how manageable is that in terms of American politics? I recall the time of President Ford's "reassessment," for example.

Circumstances have changed enormously. I would think, in terms of current American politics, the greater probability is that leadership and public opinion will turn so emphatically against Israel that reasonable Israeli positions will no longer be entertained and the long-term psychological threat to Israel will not be correctly evaluated. Certainly it is much easier for an American government to state its own position on individual issues than it was in 1975.

You don't think you're saying that just because the Sabra and Chatila massacres are so recent in the American public's memory?

No. Well before the Lebanese crisis, American leadership opinion was
moving decisively against the definitions that were commonly advanced by Jerusalem.

*Is there a similar danger — I think of Sadat's last years — of desta-
bilizing Arab regimes that we would prefer not to destabilize, by
having them associate themselves closely with compromises which
are difficult for them to make and which associate them with the current state of affairs in Israel? I think, of course, obviously of Jordan,
but also of Saudi Arabia.*

Perhaps. In my view the Camp David process played a relatively small
role in the destabilization of Sadat. The major cause was the growth
of fundamentalism in the Arab world. And also the start of a feeling
that perhaps we were shifting from Egypt to other Arab states that
had dissociated from the peace process. The question arose in some
Egyptian minds whether it had all been worth it since it seemed possible to gain all the benefits of American friendship without having run
the risks of Camp David.

That was true for Saudi Arabia. Was it true for Jordan?

No, it was true for Saudi Arabia and it was not true for Jordan only
because Jordan was not convinced enough that we could deliver.

*I wonder if fundamentalism and the peace process can be divorced
that easily in the fevered mind? Is not the American embrace an in-
citement to fundamentalists?*

Just as we have to pay attention to the intangibles of the Israeli situation, we have to take seriously the intangibles of the Arab situation
and not push friendly governments beyond the point that in everybody's best judgment is domestically tolerable.

A successful peace must be seen, first, to reflect the preferences
of at least the moderate Arab states and, second, it must move fairly
rapidly. The need for a consensus of Arab moderates is another reason why Arab states undermine themselves if they put on us the entire responsibility for the success of the peace process. As for the
second condition, insofar as the autonomy negotiations weakened

Sadat, their length and inconclusiveness was more important than their content. If the autonomy negotiations had led to a fairly rapid result . . .

Somewhere, so to speak.

Somewhere, even on terms that were questioned. So long as Sadat could have said that his method brought about some improvement in the situation where nobody else had produced anything, I think he could have enhanced his position in Egypt and even in the rest of the Arab world through the autonomy negotiations. Therefore the negotiations that are now, one hopes, about to start must be concluded in a reasonably brief period of time, say twelve to eighteen months. If they grow very prolonged, a moderate position will be cumulatively difficult to sustain and the domestic support of the participating governments will erode. Reagan's initiative must yield some tangible results while the impact of the PLO's lost military option is still fresh in everybody's mind.

It is said that American officials are disappointed in the Saudi support of the Reagan plan. Should they be?

It has been a consistent error of some of our policymakers to expect Saudi Arabia to deliver an Arab consensus. Saudi Arabia is in no position to do so; it is wise not to let itself be tempted into the complex details of the West Bank negotiations. Were we to prevail we would weaken the Kingdom without furthering the negotiation process.

Saudi Arabia faces simultaneously the uncertainties of rapid modernization and the challenges of Islamic fundamentalism. It has a secular radical neighbor to the south in the People's Democratic Republic of Yemen; a perhaps reformed but always potentially radical neighbor in Iraq to the north. Across the Gulf it faces traditional Iranian expansionism allied to religious fanaticism; across the Red Sea there is a Soviet and Cuban base in Ethiopia. The Kingdom would be tempting fate if it involved itself in all the passions of the Palestinian negotiations; it surely needs no additional enemies.

We must keep Saudi leaders informed of our plans, solicit their judgment, and take their views seriously. This dialogue will prosper in direct proportion to the discretion with which it is conducted. We may find Saudi leaders helpful where this can be done behind the scenes. To seek more is to deflect the Kingdom from what are surely our common aims: security against covetous neighbors and against radical forces within.

It was interesting to see Syria's foreign minister in Washington last month visiting President Reagan along with more moderate Arabs. Do you think that Syria is going to play the same blocking role that it has appeared to play before?

I am struck by the presence of the Syrian foreign minister in Washington and also by the interview given by the information minister, Iskandar, last month. Both of these events indicate a desire by Syria not to be left out of the negotiating process. If Syria plays a blocking role it may be more to achieve preeminence over the Palestinians than because of its objection to the concept of the settlement.

Syria usually wants a price, doesn't it, for participation, both from the Saudis in financial terms but also from others in political terms? Do you see the same pattern repeating itself?

Yes, but also Syria is now in a very difficult position because its military vulnerability has been clearly demonstrated and it cannot believe that it has a serious military option against Israel.

Is it conceivable to see Syria in any negotiations which still leave the Golan Heights not its own? Strategically, if I were the Israelis, I would want the Golan Heights long before I would want Nablus.

It is not necessary for Syria to participate in West Bank negotiations. It is enough for it to acquiesce in them. In any event, the West Bank negotiations as I envisage them are unlikely to result in a peace treaty. They can at best lead to an interim agreement of a long duration — say ten to fifteen years. As for the Golan, I have always believed that in time it is possible to make another step there in return for something like nonbelligerency that would enable Syria to maintain its principles and still participate in the process.

And Israel its security?

And Israel maintain its security by keeping a foothold on the Heights.

Jerusalem: you said earlier that it was a non-starter that it should become a UN city. That could by implication suggest that you feel that it's a non-starter that Jerusalem become internationalized in some way that allows all sides their access and pride in it.

Israel will rather go to war than abandon a united Jerusalem as its capital. I think that as part of an interim agreement something like the Vaticanization of the holy places is conceivable and would be a wise Israeli move. Again, I have no illusions about the difficulty of achieving even this much; more than that is anyhow unattainable in the initial phase of negotiations. Any attempt to go beyond that would be to invite the collapse of negotiations and the building of an Israeli consensus that would make Israelis prefer isolation, even war, to any peace process.

Since neither Camp David nor the Reagan plan envisages a comprehensive peace at this stage the negotiations which are now in prospect cannot achieve a final settlement. The best that is attainable is a long interim agreement, say ten to fifteen years. Israel would agree to new lines on the West Bank in return for nonbelligerency and precisely defined steps of normalization with at least the moderate Arab states.

A step, in other words.

Yes, but ten to fifteen years is a very long time in the Middle East. Many other things are going to happen in that period which would put matters into a new perspective.

Is it a footnote to ask you, or do you think it should be an essential part of American strategy, to conceive that, were there a favorable outcome to the kind of problems we've been discussing, greater avenues of cooperation would open up with Arab states in dealing with the threats in the Gulf?

The moderate Arab states of the Gulf must be looking now for opportunities for greater cooperation with the United States. Their self-interest is so intimately tied with American protection of both their internal structure and their borders against the danger developing from radicalism: either in the fundamentalist Iranian indigenous form or (which is not at all inconceivable to me) in the form of some domination of Iran by the Soviet Union if the Tudeh or some similar group were to succeed Khomeini. And they face a threat too from secular radical Arabs like South Yemen or even Iraq. I would look at the West Bank/Gaza negotiations not as producing a change of mind — I think the change of mind about the desirability of American cooperation has already occurred — but as making it domestically feasible for the Arabs of the Gulf to implement what they know to be necessary.

"Domestically feasible for them to implement what they know is necessary": how close an American embrace does that mean? American bases, or . . . ?

The countries in the Gulf have to understand that we are prepared to protect both their domestic structure and their frontiers; and they need to be given confidence in the means which we will use. It would be extraordinarily desirable if we could repress our tendency for publicity, and if our military could restrain their compulsion to establish a visible presence.

How do you not publicize a military base, for example?

By not establishing it. I think what we need is installations into which we could move rapidly; a physical presence near the Gulf that is plausible; and a demonstration of how we could reinforce this presence. And we must generate a credible capability for rapid support against internal upheaval. The embrace must be real and serious, but as subtle and nonpublic as possible.

I much agree with you. You don't see the negotiation on the West Bank as a precondition for that?

No, but it would ease it greatly. I can conceive that Gulf governments, despite their very best judgment, might find themselves in a position where they have to court internal collapse because they simply cannot be associated with a total failure of the West Bank negotiations.

HOW TO DEAL WITH MOSCOW

Published in Newsweek, *November 29, 1982*

THE LEADERSHIP change in the Soviet Union* — only the fourth in its sixty-five-year history — has produced much speculation about new opportunities for a breakthrough toward peace. In an age haunted by the threat of nuclear catastrophe the hope is as natural as it is necessary. Unfortunately some of the fashionable expressions of optimism are a familiar refrain heard at all previous successions. The new Soviet leader, it is said, appears to be more flexible and conciliatory than his predecessor (in this case it is because he supposedly likes Western music and reads English, hence understands us). We must strengthen, we hear, the "doves" against the "hawks" who were alleged, even in Stalin's day, to have been menacing the "reasonable and sensible and understanding" incumbent Soviet leader.

There are indeed new opportunities for peace. The 1980s may well give us a chance to make major progress with the Soviets on arms control, economic relations, and, ultimately, even on developing some ground rules for international conduct. But Yuri Andropov's fondness for American novels and Western fantasies about intrigues between hawks and doves in the Kremlin are not the sources of these opportunities. The arms race imposes dangerous uncertainties and staggering financial burdens on both parties, but especially on the Soviet Union. The recession in the West and economic stagnation in the Communist world may compel both of us to reevaluate our high levels of military spending as well as to seek mutually beneficial economic cooperation. And the increasing complexity of a world filled with regional tensions reminds both sides of the necessity of cooperation, lest a minor crisis explode into a major one, as it did in 1914.

The prospects for accord are not enhanced — they are in fact undermined — by the congenital Western tendency to psychoanalyze

* Leonid Brezhnev died on November 10, 1982; he was succeeded by Yuri Andropov.

the personality of a particular Soviet leader or to search without evidence for some faction in the Kremlin allegedly devoted to peace in the abstract. I do not pretend to know what Yuri Andropov's convictions are; I am certain that nobody in our government knows either. Only a few short weeks ago Western experts were nearly unanimous in the view that Brezhnev was the principal advocate of détente in the Kremlin — a theory to which, with qualifications, I myself subscribe. Why then should his death improve the prospects for a relaxation of tensions? How did the man who headed the Soviet secret police for fifteen years — suppressing dissidents and inventing such "humane" devices as mental hospitals for intellectual critics — suddenly emerge as a closet liberal?

Even if Andropov were such a man, the power of the general secretary of the Communist party, as it has evolved since the death of Stalin in 1953, is far from absolute — especially at the beginning of his term of office. In many fields of policy it is doubtful, in fact, that the general secretary has the discretionary power of the American President. His colleagues are suspicious, hardened by the power struggles of a lifetime. They are jealous of prerogatives that they have earned so painfully in their progress through the unwieldy bureaucracies they now control. Andropov can nudge them in his preferred direction, but any dramatic change endangers his position: Khrushchev's fate defined the risks of unorthodoxy for successors. Brezhnev, in any event, never seriously tested these limits.

To base hopes for relaxation of tensions on changes in leadership undermines the very real opportunities for diplomatic progress. It tempts the Soviet leaders into deferring the fundamental reexamination of their priorities and strategy without which the real causes of tension will continue unrelieved. And it demoralizes the democracies by trivializing the issue. We cannot ask our people to sustain the exertions and perils of a prolonged struggle if the outcome appears to depend so much on the idiosyncrasies of whoever happens to be in power in the Soviet Union.

The beginning of wisdom is therefore to recognize that there are objective causes of tension. In the last seven years we have seen Cuban troops supported by Soviet logistics in Angola and Ethiopia;

Soviet military bases in South Yemen; Soviet military equipment pouring into the rogue state of Libya; a Communist coup in Afghanistan followed by an invasion by the Soviet army; Soviet political and military support for the Vietnamese occupation of Cambodia; and Soviet intelligence support for terrorist groups in many parts of the world. All this has been buttressed by the Soviet Union's relentless military buildup, begun long before that of the Reagan Administration.

This is not to deny our own mistakes: our rhetoric has occasionally been exuberant and unrelated to sustainable strategy, our actions have sometimes been unilateral and uncoordinated with our allies, and above all we have allowed divisions both within and among the free nations. It is possible to explain this or that Soviet move as a reaction to our moves; it requires either wishful thinking or a special form of masochism to find the preponderant fault on our side or to ignore the consistent pattern of Soviet conduct which, whether by design or momentum, theatens the global equilibrium. It is this assault that must be ended if there is to be true progress toward peace.

Any serious effort to improve relations with the Soviet Union must therefore begin with an analysis of realities — those that impede progress as well as those which, properly managed, offer reason for hope. Among the factors that make for tension, ideology still plays an important role. This may sound surprising in view of the widely reported cynicism of much of the Soviet population. Nor am I suggesting that Lenin is read at bedtime by Soviet leaders as a guide to the next day's actions. The impact of ideology is more intangible: ideological élan has been replaced by an orthodox interpretation of reality; personal conviction has given way to a kind of rote impetus to undermine Western democracies and the international equilibrium. To a Leninist, peace is neither a personal affirmation nor a static condition. It reflects "objective factors" — the balance of power, the state of the economy or technology. No Soviet leader, for example, can justify concessions on the basis of the personal goodwill or sincerity of a Western leader. Soviet negotiators make concessions to what they define as the balance of forces, not to personalities. They understand concrete proposals based on reciprocity; unilateral gestures are likely to be interpreted as a trick or as a confession of weakness. It is no accident that those presidents most eager for an improvement of relations, most prone to personalize their diplomacy, and most resistant to the concept of balance of power suffered a shipwreck with the Kremlin; while those presidents who were least sentimental and insisted on strict reciprocity were the most successful. Absent a balance of forces *and* a concrete Western program for peace, all pressures within the Soviet society make for a continuation of the present course, if only as a result of philosophical and institutional rigidity.

There are some American conservatives in both parties who luxuriate in the myth of diabolic Soviet planners implementing a detailed master plan for world revolution. No one who has actually dealt with the top Soviet leadership has encountered such types. If they exist, they are well hidden from foreign visitors. The leaders one in fact encounters are tough, ruthless, and persistent. But they have originated no profound initiatives; they have usually avoided great risks. They have expanded into vacuums created by irresolution or weakness. They have systematically accumulated power not in support of a predetermined plan for aggression but rather because the notion that there may be an upper limit of usable power is foreign to them, and instinct leads them to believe that strength is directly translatable into bargaining position and political advantage.

Bureaucratic inertia reinforces ideological proclivity. The irony of Communist systems is that they contain the seeds of Bonapartism. For the sole organizations outside the Communist party with autonomous command structures are the armed forces and the paramilitary units — some 200,000 men strong — of the KGB. One way or another the armed forces emerged as balance wheels in the struggles among the hierarchs of the party; in Poland they have become the heirs of its disintegration, in the Soviet Union the head of the secret police has taken over. Since no one can achieve eminence — much less the top spot — without military or paramilitary support, these forces are in a position to exact constantly increasing resources. The growth of Soviet military power is built into the system — if only as a result of internecine power struggles. If not matched by the West, this military expansion will inevitably create temptations for blackmail since Communist ideology has no rationale for not exploiting a favorable power balance.

Only overriding necessity can alter this rhythm. Fortunately such conditions are likely to appear during the eighties. If Western policy is firm and creative, the Soviet leadership will have every incentive to consider alternatives. For one thing, Soviet foreign policy has not been a startling success. It has been said, and not only as a joke, that the Soviet Union is the only country in the world entirely surrounded by hostile Communist states. The satellite orbit is an economic drain and in Poland a demonstration of political as well as economic bankruptcy. Afghanistan is a festering wound. China — whatever temporary tactical adjustments are made — is in the long term a geopolitical nightmare as its billion people modernize along a distant, disputed frontier 4,000 miles long. Lebanon has shown the near-irrelevance of Soviet power and influence in the Arab-Israeli conflict. The Soviet adventure in Africa has led to no breakthrough. Growing pacifism in some European countries is balanced by the advent of a conservative government in Germany and by declining Communist strength in France and Spain.

Moreover, the Soviet Union will not be able to evade much longer the contradictions between the necessities of a modern industrialized society and the rigidities of the Communist system. What institution in the West could survive with no method for replacing a governing board whose average age is over seventy? Where there is no constitutional procedure, loyalty goes to the person, not to the office; power is exercised in a ruthlessly competitive struggle for survival. Leaders dare not relinquish the positions that ensure their power and subordinates dare not urge change because their personal fate is tied to their patron. The trend is toward gerontocracy. It is no accident that each successive general secretary has come from an age group ten years older than his predecessor. Stalin was in his forties when he succeeded to office; Khrushchev was in his fifties; Brezhnev was in his sixties by the time he eclipsed Kosygin; Andropov will be at least seventy before he consolidates his power. His rule will be shadowed from the beginning by the relative imminence of a new succession.

The Soviet system is also an economic disaster. To run a large modern economy by central planning is to institutionalize backwardness and inefficiency. Ironically, the attempt to achieve total predictability leads to near-absolute arbitrariness. Where managers can choose neither customers nor supplies, all incentives work the wrong way. Managers deliberately underestimate their capacity lest the failure to reach an ambitious target reflect on their political reliability. Since they cannot influence allocations except by bureaucratic maneuvers outside the economic process, they will hoard labor and materials at the cost of productivity — to avoid being caught short by sudden bottlenecks outside their control. Thus the paradoxes of the Soviet economy: shortages and surpluses exist side by side, and congenitally inferior goods are produced with no relation to the desires of its people. It is an amazing phenomenon — a superpower whose intercontinental missiles terrify the world cannot produce a single industrial commodity competitive with the products of even newly developed market economies like South Korea and Singapore, not to speak of the mature industrial democracies of Western Europe, Japan, Canada, and the United States.

These incongruities affect Soviet relationships to the outside world in several ways. They reinforce Soviet leaders' determination to insulate their people from contact with other societies, to keep them from making unfavorable comparisons. They require the invocation of constant foreign dangers to explain the backwardness of a system claiming to represent the forces of history yet unable to demonstrate progress to its average citizens. And finally — and perhaps crucially — economic stagnation must raise serious doubts in the minds of some Soviet leaders whether the country's security is compatible over the long term with an unrestrained arms race.

The Soviet military buildup of the sixties and seventies occurred from a low base, with relatively simple technology, during a period of steady economic growth. This may not be sustainable in the eighties and nineties except by efforts that distort the Soviet economy even further. The performance of Soviet weapons in Lebanon could be an augury. Weapons that had exacted a serious toll in Vietnam and the 1973 Middle East war proved almost totally vulnerable to American technology and Israeli skill. This not only weakened the Soviet position in the Middle East; it also devalued the single most important Soviet export. If the Soviets continue to refuse a realistic downturn in the arms race, they doom themselves to repeating the whole anguishing cycle of austerity and weapons development under new, much more difficult, and far more problematical circumstances.

In that sense Brezhnev's last major speech, expressing to his generals his determination not to fall behind in technology, had something of the quality of whistling in a graveyard. For it is inconceivable that the Soviet defense establishment had not already devoted every available resource to military research and development. Shortcomings in Soviet technology cannot be remedied by pep talks; they almost certainly require a structural change in the Soviet economy.

This leads to another unsolved Soviet dilemma: what to do with a Communist party that has no function except to champion a discredited ideology and to preserve its own power? The Communist party is not needed either for administration or for economic management, yet it dominates both without contributing to either. Communists in Communist societies are turning into an elite of privileged supernumeraries with a vested interest in prolonging crises they cannot resolve. And all this occurs against the background of an ominous sociological fact: in the foreseeable future the non-Russian population of the Soviet Union will be a majority, raising new problems of political reliability and productivity.

The Soviet Union remains formidable. No abstract dedication to peace, no counterpart to the Western peace movements will impel those hardened analysts of objective factors to reassess their course. But the instinct for self-preservation of Soviet leaders should lead at least some of them to the conclusion that the country is overextended and must somewhere retrench. This is not psychology; it is reality. Therein lies our opportunity for a diplomatic breakthrough.

The diplomatic opportunity will not present itself unambiguously or painlessly. The Soviet leaders will not easily turn to structural reform or to fundamental negotiations. They will surely prefer the easier way out, which is to tranquilize us by conciliatory rhetoric while continuing to amass arms and maintaining the diplomatic status quo. They will try to gain maneuvering room by peace offensives aimed at Europe and a relaxation with China. They will almost surely seek to tempt us with high-level meetings ending in ringing declarations and peripheral measures. If the West appears too confused and divided, they may even be tempted into military adventures to reduce the external threat before turning to domestic reform.

All this is within our power to prevent. To bring about a genuine change — expressed in substantial reciprocal arms reduction and restraint in international conduct — requires American leadership founded in firm purpose, clear concept, and steadfast strategy. The West will lose its opportunity for peace if it tempts the Soviets into the belief that we will hand them their objectives through our own exhaustion, self-righteousness, and obsession with public relations. There are worrisome trends in this regard. Military and arms control policy are now at loggerheads. I support an increase in our defense spending, but the current program provides increases in many categories of weapons without a cohesive rationale for how they relate to each other or to an overall defense strategy. What rationale is advanced tends to be based on comparisons with Soviet weapons, rather than on the objectives that our different geography and resources ought to dictate.

Most strategic analysts favor a shift of emphasis to conventional weapons; church groups stigmatize nuclear weapons; and yet Congress presses for a reduction of our military spending. All of this will make a continued reliance on a nuclear strategy inevitable, while undermining the psychological base for it. The West could thus be heading for a form of unilateral disarmament while sitting on the most destructive arsenal the world has seen. Clearly this lessens the Soviet incentives for serious negotiations.

On the pipeline issue, the Administration asked the right question: should the West contribute to the technological development of the Soviet Union without insisting on some linkage to restrained geopolitical conduct? But tying sanctions to Poland only obscured this more basic issue, which would have had to have been confronted whatever happened to Solidarity. The promised studies of the East-

West trade problem can lead to a more unified strategy of economic diplomacy only if our allies do not use them solely to gain time to tranquilize us and if we, for our part, are prepared to include measures that will require sacrifice from us as well, such as limiting grain sales. Both arms control and trade policy need to be freed of the penchant for spasmodic one-shot action and must be made part of a coherent national security strategy.

The United States must learn to combine military strength with a strategy for peace. A positive diplomatic program is the prerequisite for maintaining public and allied support for a strong defense and foreign policy. It could help us avoid the danger that our body politic will be torn between peace movements advocating forms of escapism and official policies neither supported nor understood by our public. Alternating bellicose rhetoric with sudden concessions only raises doubts about our steadiness among supporters and will be dismissed as mere tactics by opponents. The United States should not be reluctant to make the opening move. Every successful East-West negotiation in the postwar period has resulted from American proposals. Conservative critics cite this as a sign of the West's tendency toward appeasement. And it is true that the free countries' impatience with deadlock enables the Soviets occasionally simply to sit back and elicit even more favorable Western offers. But this is particularly true if the public debate turns on whether to negotiate at all.

If, however, we preempt the negotiating process with a bold program, we have a chance to dominate both diplomacy and public discussion. Soviet bureaucratic rigidity is hostile to imagination — in diplomacy as in other fields. Not infrequently they are better placed to respond with a counterproposal than to originate an offer. We should seize every opportunity to put before them negotiating proposals that reflect *our* definitions of genuine arms control, proper economic relations, and restrained international conduct. It can only be to our advantage to negotiate from our agenda, not theirs.

Thoughtful, concrete proposals prosper better in quiet diplomacy than in dramatic public presentations that invite a propaganda battle. We must persevere in them for the time it takes to test the real, not the propagandistic, Soviet reaction. They must reflect a clear view of our own purposes, including what we will not accept. Our policy must be based on strength to discourage adventurism yet at the same time offer a vision of a better world for all peoples, including the peoples of the Soviet Union.

At home this requires an armistice in the debate that has rent our country for over a decade — between those extreme conservatives who reject all negotiations as a trap and every agreement as a surrender and those extreme liberals who insist that most of our dangers are self-induced, to be remedied by unremitting pressure on our own government. The Administration has the obligation to put forward an intelligible strategy for dealing with the Soviet Union. Until now it has alternated intransigent assaults on a caricature of the détente policy of the 1970s with sweeping gestures better suited to fend off pressures than to achieve any permanent result.

But while the Administration — as all new administrations — could benefit from great coherence, it deserves recognition for having created the building blocks of a promising foreign policy. Its firm tone has prevented major Soviet challenges. Beneath the often exuberant rhetoric, the Administration's actions have almost invariably been restrained and responsible. The major need is to relate the pieces to each other and to place them under unified strategic and tactical control. There exists, then, every reason for reconciliation.

Without reconciliation there can be no continuity. Without continuity we risk growing irrelevant. Americans do not always understand to what extent our freewheeling process of arriving at decisions unsettles those who have staked their political survival on us. When a foreign statesman follows our lead, he ties his reputation to our judgment. When we reverse course, we in effect undermine him. This happens almost across the board when administrations change and, too frequently, even within administrations. The history of SALT and of various weapons deployments is replete with examples of key foreign leaders having been left high and dry by sudden and unilateral American reversals of positions. Over time they will seek to free themselves of such risks, thereby reducing our influence and pushing us to the sidelines.

It is equally crucial and more difficult to create a consensus among allies. Right now the allies are divided over the assessment of Soviet conduct, military strategy, important aspects of arms control, and many issues outside the NATO area. These divisions invite the Soviets to apply détente selectively in order to split the West so that it can avoid having to face its own dilemmas. It is in fact conceivable that Soviet leaders can project Western disintegration as a mirror image of Soviet trends described earlier; in that case they will seek to outwait us.

Whether this happens is largely up to us. The West is in the fortunate position that its problems — major as they are — almost without exception can be remedied by a new effort of unity, coherence, and will on the part of the democracies. The Soviet Union cannot make this claim; its problems are systematic, structural, and fundamental. If we can rally ourselves and develop a vision of a better future, a broad and comprehensive East-West negotiation could be within our grasp.

SAVING THE WORLD ECONOMY

Published in Newsweek, *January 24, 1983*

JOHN MAYNARD KEYNES wrote that practical men who believe themselves quite exempt from intellectual influences are usually the slaves of some defunct economist. Politicians these days certainly have many economic theories to choose from; most discordant, not a few of them defunct. No previous theory seems capable of explaining the current crisis of the world economy. Until recently it would have been thought impossible that prices could rise during a recession; that a system of relatively free trade and floating exchange rates could spur embryonic trade wars; that the developing nations, through defaulting on their debts, could threaten the economies of the industrial nations.

When reality clashes fundamentally with expectations, a political crisis is inevitable. That condition is upon us today. Since World War II we have expected progress. The historical business cycle of boom and bust seemed a relic of history. In virtually every Western nation the standard of living rose uninterrupted. Jobs were so plentiful that many countries encouraged the immigration of foreign labor. Although the developing countries lagged far behind, the more advanced among them — such as Brazil, Mexico, and South Korea — were beginning to share in the seemingly permanent prosperity.

This illusion of uninterrupted progress was suddenly shattered in the middle seventies. There were many causes: the welfare state grew dramatically faster than productivity; inflation accelerated; high taxation reduced incentives; a generation of economic security eroded the work ethic. But what transformed these structural problems into a crisis was the more than tenfold increase in oil prices between 1973 and 1980. At first it drove inflation out of control and — when governments put on correspondingly severe brakes — it triggered global recession. Thirty million workers are now unemployed in the industrial democracies and their number continues to increase. The developing nations are crushed under the twin burden of debt and collapsing hopes of progress.

No government of an industrial democracy has survived an election since the conditions became chronic. Socialist or liberal governments in West Germany, Britain, and the United States have been replaced by conservative ones; conservative governments in France, Greece, Spain, and Sweden have been succeeded by socialist ones. The common feature is not the program of the parties but the condition of the societies; restlessness with a recession that seems to have neither remedy nor end; fear of a future to which there are no signposts.

If the peoples of the West lose faith that democratic governments have control over their economic destinies, the economic crisis could become a crisis of Western democracy. Each country will turn inward to protect its immediate patrimony, eroding cooperation and paradoxically deepening the world recession. In a world of many perils, continuing economic weakness is likely to undermine the democracies' ability to conduct an effective foreign policy or to maintain their collective defense.

Historians will never settle conclusively whether the economic policies of the New Deal overcame the crisis of the 1930s or delayed its resolution. But Franklin Delano Roosevelt has earned his place among our great presidents not because of his economic theories but because he restored confidence in the ability of our democratic institutions to master their difficulties. Today's crisis poses a comparable challenge. Now, as then, the first reaction is to cut consumption, reduce imports, and expand exports. Now, as then, purely economic measures will not work.

In the first place, economic recovery through austerity almost surely will take longer than the citizens of most advanced democracies will tolerate; in the developing world, austerity may cause political chaos. More important, a remedy appropriate for the economic ills of one nation may prove self-defeating if applied by many nations at once. If many nations simultaneously reduce consumption and imports and boost exports, none can possibly succeed. Trade will be stifled, recession will be institutionalized, and the risks of political instability compounded.

Before this downward cycle goes too far, the governments of the industrial democracies must reverse the process. They must promote economic growth, and they can do so only in coordination; solitary efforts are bound to fail.

If we do not act, we face many risks, including the loss of the relatively free international trading system that was the basis of postwar prosperity. Contrary to classical economic theory, a free-trading system does not run itself; it requires a conscious act of political leadership. In the best of circumstances that task is formidable; deep recession makes it next to impossible.

THE POLITICS OF FREE TRADE

In theory free trade benefits everybody. Tariffs and other trade barriers, it is said, encourage inefficiency, restrict commerce, and lower the general standard of living. But the theory of free trade is rooted in a world that no longer exists. Adam Smith first advanced it in 1776, when Great Britain had a near-monopoly in industrialization. Competition benefited some British industries and not others, but it did not affect Britain's total employment. As other nations industrialized (almost invariably behind temporary tariff walls), free trade prospered because there were abundant world markets and only a few key nations — no more than four or five — representing homogeneous cultures with comparable living standards operating by the discipline of the gold standard.

Today's world economy, by contrast, contains at least twenty significant trading nations of widely different cultural backgrounds with great variations in labor costs and standards of living, each claiming sovereign control over its economic decisions. In such conditions, competition became more ruthless and its impact more drastic. No longer does one sector of industry within one country benefit at the expense of another; rather, whole industries decline simultaneously or even move from one country to another. The problems of our steel and automobile industries require no elaboration; very few television sets are still made in the United States. Many European countries with high expenditures for social welfare and inflexible labor costs are in an even more difficult position.

All political pressures and incentives of the modern democratic state work against the acceptance of the bitter medicine of government-sponsored austerity and cutthroat foreign competition. The loss of jobs sets up fierce pressures for protectionism. Nearly all industrial democracies — even while they give lip service to the ideals of free trade — have sought to nudge the terms of trade in a nationalist direction. Subsidies of exports, nontariff barriers to imports, guaranteed credits, as well as the manipulation of exchange rates, become the order of the day. While one or two nations can occasionally manipulate the free-trading system to their advantage, the attempt by all nations to do so will surely wreck it.

The hope for recovery of a cooperative world order depends on the preservation of the free-trading system. The industrial democracies must either agree to adhere to the principles of free trade — or else they will live in a mercantilistic world of unilateral actions and bilateral deals. At the same time, the free-trading system will not survive in a world of chronic recession. There is no hope of resisting the tide of protectionism unless the world returns to a path of economic growth.

But recovery will not take place if different countries in the industrialized world continue to pursue incompatible economic policies. America, as the strongest country, must take the lead. It cannot do so, however, in isolation. The industrial democracies must achieve an unprecedented coordination of their national economic policies. No single American initiative would more effectively reverse the deterioration of the Western Alliance than a call for a coordinated program to ensure the general economic expansion of the free world. Nothing is more likely to encourage a sound political evolution in the developing countries than the hope that they may share soon in renewed growth. And nothing would more effectively strengthen our hand with our adversaries than the assurance that the democratic world has dedicated itself to the recovery of economic strength.

EXCHANGE-RATE POLITICS

Perhaps no other field so dramatically illustrates the changing fashions in economic theory and its growing incompatibility with political practice than the current system of international exchange rates. Throughout the nineteenth century currencies were stable; prices in 1914 were essentially unchanged from 1812. The gold standard gave political leaders an alibi for self-discipline. And even when the gold standard was abandoned after World War I, nations fixed their exchange rates by formal agreement.

As recently as 1969, fixed exchange rates were still an article of faith. I remember a meeting of Cabinet-level officials when someone suggested a change in the value of the dollar. He was never given a chance to put forward his case. It was explained to him — with the forced patience of the exasperated — that the dollar as a reserve currency *had* to have a fixed value; indeed, it was technically impossible either to revalue or to devalue it, for all other currencies would simply follow suit.

Within a few years intellectual fashion had made a 180-degree turn. By 1973 a totally new system of floating exchange rates emerged from largely unilateral American actions. The new rules made possible — indeed, encouraged — continuous changes in the value of all currencies. The value of currencies was no longer fixed; the market was supposed to determine it. No country, it was held, would tolerate an overvalued currency because it reduces the competitiveness of exports, or an undervalued one because it creates inflationary pressures. When the value of their currency changed, governments were expected to take immediate remedial action.

Unfortunately, practice belied theory; far from establishing discipline the floating system tended to erode it. When currencies weaken, exports thrive; for a country eager to sell abroad, the incentive to remedy this state of affairs is minimal. Some major trading nations — Japan is the prime example — have even been accused of deliberately maintaining an undervalued currency. Other countries have overvalued their currency to serve domestic policies. The United States, for example, has relied on high interest rates to fight inflation, thus boosting demands for the dollar. The remedy was successful —

at least in the short run — but the consequence was to drain the world's liquidity, reduce global investment, and weaken the competitiveness of American products, both at home and abroad.

In short, unilateral decisions regarding exchange rates have profoundly affected the world economy and the well-being of many countries that had no part in them. Unpredictability encourages speculation; the system tempts imbalances instead of adjusting them. A new form of nationalistic competition evolves, all the more bitter for never having to be made explicit; the floating system encourages the myth that governments make no decisions at all.

An overhaul of the international monetary system is therefore a precondition to world economic recovery. Secretary of the Treasury Donald Regan's suggestions for reform are an important start; they need to be translated into specific initiatives. While a more fundamental reform is being negotiated, the central banks could in the meantime agree on a realistic range for permissible exchange-rate fluctuations and take action when relationships among major currencies move outside this range. Reform of exchange markets and practices is only a partial step. Monetary reform, like free trade, will not succeed without the coordination of fiscal and monetary policies to prevent the imbalances that give rise to the misalignment of currencies in the first place.

OPEC'S OMINOUS LEGACY

Any serious effort to restore the world economy must come to grips with the massive debts of the developing nations and the threat they pose to the international economic and political order. There is a special irony here. For the better part of a decade, the developing countries have been insisting on a massive transfer of resources in the name of what they called a New International Economic Order. The industrial democracies have either rejected or evaded the proposal. Now it transpires that a vast and virtually unnoticed transfer of resources has in fact been undertaken by the much-maligned capitalist banking system on a scale that not even the most enthusiastic advocates of official aid would have dared to propose.

The energy crisis of the 1970s has turned into a parable on the fallibility of human foresight. Each party acting perfectly reasonably in response to immediate pressures nevertheless created an almost insoluble complexity. The oil producers, suddenly awash in dollars, placed their surpluses into Western commercial banks, usually in the form of short-term deposits The banks, flush with resources unimaginable even a few years earlier, competed fiercely for long-term loans to developing countries — especially to the more advanced countries of Latin America. Governments encouraged the process of "recycling" the petrodollars in order to maintain the oil producers' incentive to pump oil and also to foster the economic growth of the developing world. The passiveness of government and the competitiveness of the banks solved an immediate problem by mortgaging the future. When the short-term deposits of the oil producers were converted into the long-term lending of the banks, the Western financial system became enormously vulnerable.

The industrial democracies have therefore wound up paying for the energy crisis three times: first in the inflation and recession induced by high oil prices; then in the inflationary pressures arising from the massive extension of credit to help developing nations; and finally in the threat to the Western financial system caused by the inability of the developing nations to repay their debts.

The developing countries face a comparable triple jeopardy. First, the rising oil prices consumed most if not all of the official aid extended to them. Next, the high interest rates caused by the oil-price increases made it impossible to repay the commercial debt that served as a supplement to official aid. Now they confront an austerity from which even stable oil prices may not be able to extricate them. Falling oil prices help energy-importing countries like Brazil; they spell potential disaster to overextended oil-producing debtors like Mexico, Nigeria, or Venezuela.

The wealthy oil producers are free of debt, but caught in the vicious circle as well. They have geared their development budgets to rising oil prices. Now that prices are stable and even declining, they are left with a budgetary deficit that they meet by drawing down their balances in Western banks. But this reduces the funds available to help the non-oil-producing developing countries through their debt crisis.

In 1982 interest payments alone ranged up to 45 percent of the total exports of goods and services of the developing countries. An attempt to repay principal — amounting to some $500 billion — would increase that percentage substantially. These figures spell a crisis. The debtor countries cannot possibly earn enough to meet their present obligations, at least for so long as the recession continues and probably for long afterward.

Creditors and debtors are thus bound together in a system in which disaster for one side spells ruin for the other. The creditor cannot cut the debtor off from further aid without risking not only a banking disaster but also a deepening of the recession. The developing countries, after all, absorb more than one-third of US exports (and more than 40 percent of the exports of the industrial democracies). For the United States this is more than we export to the European Community and Japan combined.

Because the debtors can never escape their plight unless they receive additional credits, the comforting view has developed that no debtor country would dare default and wreck its creditworthiness. Unfortunately political leaders march to a different drummer than financial experts. They see the political interests of their country through the prism of their own survival. If pushed into a corner, a political leader may well seek to rally populist resentment against foreign "exploiters." This will surely occur if the so-called rescue operation concentrates primarily on the repayment of interest. A blowup is certain sooner or later if debtor countries are asked to accept prolonged austerity simply to protect the balance sheets of foreign banks.

The key question thus becomes: what is the likely impact on the political structure of the debtor country of the conditions demanded for "rescheduling," or stretching out, its debt payment? At risk here is the internal political evolution of several developing countries, including many important friends of the United States. If the debt crisis winds up spawning radical anti-Western governments, the financial issues will be overwhelmed by the political consequences.

Of course it would be absurd for the International Monetary Fund (IMF) to launch a rescue operation without seeking to correct the economic practices that brought debtor nations to the edge of the precipice. But the conditions imposed must be relevant to the real problem. How meaningful, for example, is the commitment to austerity of an Argentine military government daily losing legitimacy and in the process of turning over its authority to civilians of a quite different political orientation? With the best of intentions, can these targets be met? And if not, what incentive does such a government have to refrain from a politically popular repudiation of debt?

But the IMF conditions can be even more dangerous when they *are* fulfilled. For then, the debtor country may undermine itself politically. Western governments in economic trouble have occasionally used conditions imposed by international lenders as an excuse to practice an austerity that domestic politics might otherwise have prevented — Britain in late 1976 is a good example. In most developing countries, however, prolonged austerity is bound to shake, perhaps to shatter, the legitimacy of political structures that are the principal expressions of national cohesion and identity.

Few debtor nations have unemployment insurance or other institutions that in the West cushion the social impact of economic downturns. A policy of forcing developing countries to reduce their standard of living drastically over a long period is likely to weaken precisely those moderate governments that are the most likely to accept Western advice. If pushed too far it risks provoking radicalism that will rally public opinion (and perhaps other debtors) by defying foreign creditors. This must be the opposite of the West's intent.

Existing international arrangements are hardly well designed to recognize this danger, much less deal with it. The principal institution for overcoming the liquidity and repayment crisis of the debtor nations is the IMF. But the IMF's original purpose was to lend to individual countries that found themselves in temporary difficulty. The IMF has performed this function admirably. But the IMF was *not* designed to deal with a crisis of the system affecting scores of debtor nations simultaneously.

As country after country admits its inability to pay even interest — and therefore renounces any immediate prospect of repaying capital — the IMF will quickly discover that it does not have the resources to rescue the entire developing world. But even an increase in its resources — and in recent weeks the United States has thrown its weight behind the effort to beef up the IMF's available funds — cannot cure the inherent contradiction in the IMF's basic strategy. As a condition for its assistance, the IMF almost invariably insists on measures that have the effect of contracting the economy, increasing unemployment, and reducing consumption, in order to slow imports and shift resources to exports. The problem is that IMF conditions cannot work if applied at the same time in many countries, particularly in a period of global recession.

Above all, austerity in a developing nation is politically bearable only if rapid progress can be shown toward an escape from the vicious circle in which debt service consumes export earnings. The heart of the problem is that the current rescue effort pretends to "solve" a debt problem that is in fact insoluble in the immediate future. In the process it does provide an excuse for banks to continue lending. But our real objective must be to promote a sustained process of growth in the developing world; without it, all the frantic activity of rescheduling is simply delaying the inevitable crisis.

The first step must be to change the bargaining framework; the debtors should be deprived — to the extent possible — of the weapon of default. The industrial democracies urgently require a safety net permitting some emergency governmental assistance to threatened financial institutions. This would reduce both the sense of panic and the debtor's capacity for blackmail. At the same time it would permit a more farsighted approach to the debt crisis focusing on the long-term growth of the developing world. Simultaneously, new crisis machinery should be created. The IMF needs an early-warning system and advance consultation among the principal lenders so that crises can be anticipated and prevented. But in the end the issue is psychological. The debt problem is the symptom, not the cause, of a structural crisis. The developing world must be given hope for a better future if it is to sustain the immediate and inevitable austerity without convulsions.

THE CHALLENGES TO AMERICA

Only America can lead the world to rapid economic recovery, and we cannot fulfill this role without a long-term economic strategy. The free market is the most successful mechanism of producing prosperity and freedom. But the free market alone will not overcome the present economic crisis. The government must play a crucial role. We need clear decisions in at least two crucial domestic areas relevant to foreign policy.

The first is energy. There are powerful national security reasons for reducing our dependence on foreign oil, and with it the risk of blackmail. But with oil prices stable or declining, there is little incentive for the large investments needed for systematic development of alternative sources of energy — even though it is all but certain that within the decade the energy crisis will return. When the recession ends, demands will increase; the Persian/Arabian Gulf has surely not seen its last political convulsion. In addition, some oil-producing countries will deplete their reserves. The oil glut is temporary, a breathing space for the democracies to insure themselves against future crises. Since current market conditions do not encourage the necessary investments, the government should provide the incentives to encourage alternative sources — as well as creation of strategic oil reserves.

Similarly, if we are serious about free trade, we have an obligation to cushion some of its harmful consequences on our people. International competition and automation can no longer be counted on to create more jobs than they abolish, as theorists used to assure us. High unemployment may in fact become chronic even after the recession ends. And as unemployment reaches the white-collar labor force, discontent may spread to the middle class whose frustrations have historically been the breeding ground of extremism and rampant nationalism. If we prize either domestic or international stability, a conscious strategy to ease the adjustment process is therefore imperative — including programs of retraining, emergency assistance, and tax incentives and other measures to encourage the flow of resources to the sectors with the most potential for growth.

Finally, it is not too early to prepare a fall-back position, in case we and the other industrial democracies fail to coordinate our economic policies; we may then have no choice except to prepare to ensure our competitive survival — deliberately and systematically — in the rough new world of unilateral trade practices and bilateral arrangements that is sure to follow.

This agenda will require a major change in the role of our government. Government, industry, and labor must act as partners in setting the broad outlines of a national strategy, which should then be maintained on a bipartisan basis. Of the industrial democracies only Japan has managed this tour de force, and its national strategy is one reason for Japan's competitive edge in world markets.

In the immediate postwar period the Marshall Plan saved the European democracies by offering the vision of a better world. Sacrifice was sustained by hope. The United States faces a comparable challenge today, both toward the industrial democracies and toward the moderate countries of the developing world. Clemenceau said that war is too serious an affair to be left to generals. By the same token the current global economic crisis is too grave to be left to financial experts. The political and moral impetus to restore hope to Western economies must come from the heads of state and their foreign ministers. For the stakes are high: whether the economic system as we have known it will hold together — as well as the political relationships that go with it. The next economic summit at Williamsburg — or perhaps a less public forum — could serve as the launching pad for a new policy.

Nearly two centuries ago the German philosopher Immanuel Kant predicted that eventually world order would come about either through intellectual and moral insight or through the experience of chaos. We are still in a position to make that choice. If the United States does not lead, we will sooner rather than later be confronting a panicky stampede. If we seize the initiative, we can draw from uncertainty and incipient despair an act of creation. And this, after all, is how almost all great creations have come about.

MR. SHULTZ GOES TO CHINA
What Should Come Out of This Trip

Published in The Washington Post,
January 30, 1983

SINO-AMERICAN relations have been on a roller coaster for the past generation. In World War II and its immediate aftermath, America somewhat sentimentally tried to promote a weak China, torn by civil war, to great-power status. Then, with the Chinese revolution and the Korean war, came a swing to the other extreme of seemingly permanent hostility, with contact between the two countries to all intents and purposes broken off. When a rapprochement finally took place in the early 1970s, many Americans fell prey to our nostalgic national habit of equating relations among states with relations among people and endowed it with qualities of personal friendship.

In the nature of things, this raised exaggerated expectations that could not be fulfilled. Almost inevitably, strains have developed. To some extent occasional squabbles are a sign of maturation, of a normal relationship between countries. Still, the tensions in recent years have gained their own momentum, threatening to damage the important common long-term objectives of both countries.

It is to reverse this process that Secretary of State George Shultz has set out on his journey.

Conventional wisdom has it that the current difficulties are largely due to the clumsiness of the Reagan Administration. To be sure, some of the exuberant early statements on Taiwan will not be landmarks in the annals of diplomatic finesse, and the unpropitious timing of the textile issue just prior to the Shultz visit makes one wonder about the coordinating mechanism in our government.

The fact remains that the Administration has gone to extraordinary lengths — even more remarkable given its starting point — to emphasize its commitment to close ties with Peking. And it took two to make the textile issue intractable. The causes of the strains in

Washington-Peking relations go deeper; they antedate the Reagan Administration; they have been exacerbated in both countries by errors of judgment and domestic conflicts.

These strains originate, indeed, in the two countries' differing approaches to foreign policy. During the early period of renewed contacts, much innocent nonsense could be heard about how "unnatural" had been the estrangement between the American and the Chinese peoples, as if rapprochement fulfilled a deep emotional necessity on both sides. The facts were far more prosaic. China, in its marvelous history of 3,000 years, has never had the experience of dealing with other societies on the basis of equality. It has felt most comfortable when able to be aloof, self-contained, as a culture whose uniqueness placed it beyond the reach of outsiders.

For China there was nothing at all unnatural about living apart from America. Nor can it be said that in 1971 there was a ground-swell of grass-roots demand in the United States for an opening to China.

What brought the two nations together was not sentiment but awareness of a common threat. The Chinese saw an awesome buildup of Soviet military power along the border, including nuclear missiles and forty modern combat divisions. By 1969, it was obvious to China that Marxist theory not only did not shield it from military pressures; on the contrary, the newly promulgated "Brezhnev doctrine" claimed the right to enforce the unity of the Communist world by military might.

For the United States, opportunity combined with necessity. The expansion of Soviet military power and constant Soviet pressures on the international equilibrium had been for us a familiar feature of the postwar scene. But it was only in the late 1960s that the United States began to sense the limits of its power and to recognize the need for associations beyond our traditional allies. The process was given impetus by a sophisticated President to whom an unsentimental perception of power relationships was congenial rather than anathema. There were powerful incentives for a rapprochement with China: to balance the Soviet Union, either to restrain it or to induce it to negotiate seriously; to isolate Hanoi to give it an incentive to end the Viet-

nam war; to maintain American self-assurance amid our messy withdrawal from Indochina by demonstrating our continuing capacity for
major positive initiatives.

The new links between China and America flourished so long as
the two sides kept their eye on the common objective of resisting what
their communiqués came to describe as "hegemony." Simply put, this
meant resistance to Soviet attempts to overturn the global balance of
power and some agreement on an appropriate strategy to achieve this
end.

There were inevitable differences in tactical perspective. In the
developing world, Peking often relied on competing with Moscow in
appealing to radical movements, which led it to back some leaders
and causes that were hardly America's favorites. Also, China was
leery of Washington's relations with Moscow, explicitly fearful that
détente would undermine the West's willingness to stand up to the
Soviet Union, implicitly suspicious that it might lead to a US–Soviet
arrangement at China's expense.

These differences were downgraded early on because each side
had an interest in rapid and visible progress — the United States to
demonstrate its new options amidst the frustrations of the Vietnam
war; China to discourage the Soviet Union from attempting to apply
the "Brezhnev doctrine" to it. Thus both sides strove to achieve a coordination of purposes if not of policies. High-level Chinese-American
meetings were unique in that they rarely concerned concrete or technical negotiations; most of the conversations dealt with basic geopolitical assessments, projects, and strategies. In the touchy field of
Washington's relations with Moscow, the United States took great
pains to keep Peking fully informed. In this manner, tactical differences were kept in perspective and not allowed to harm the essentials
of Sino–US relations. In that process, interestingly enough, our relations with the Soviet Union prospered as well.

The succeeding years made this mutual restraint increasingly
difficult to maintain. Domestic upheavals preoccupied the leaders of
both countries and spilled over into foreign policy. At first, relations
with Moscow were at the heart of the problem. The United States always had a difficult passage to navigate: if Washington grew too exu-

berant about détente, we would disquiet Peking and stampede it into
its own overtures to Moscow in order to avoid being left at the gate. If
we were too intransigent, Peking might take our counterbalancing of
Moscow for granted and be tempted to flaunt opposition to us on bilateral issues or in some areas of the world without fear of being left
alone with the Soviet Union.

The Carter Administration oscillated between both extremes.
The Vance wing gave clear priority to improving relations with Moscow; the Brzezinski wing spoke of a "China card" as if Peking were a
weapon in our arsenal. But a card can be discarded as well as played;
the unintended consequence was the unnerving inference that, for the
right price from Moscow, we might loosen our ties with Peking.

The Reagan Administration suffered from no such ambivalence.
Its anti-Soviet pronouncements seemed to freeze us into a rigid hostility toward the Soviet Union, which freed China to adopt, at little
risk, a militant Third World posture of "a plague on both your
houses." At the same time, some members of the new Administration
expressed philosophic convictions very different from those of their
predecessors with respect to China itself and its relationship to Taiwan, causing Peking to fear (incorrectly) a regression to the Dulles
era.

Nor is the fault all on the American side. Since the first American visit to China, Peking has experienced major domestic upheavals
of its own. It would be astonishing if China's internal political battles
remained confined to the publicized issues. Inevitably, some of the
stridency in the reaction to American policies reflected, at least in
part, factional rivalries exploiting the presumed embarrassments of
Chinese leaders at not obtaining greater or more rapid concessions
from the United States. In recent years, the Taiwan issue — which is
genuinely neuralgic for the Chinese — has nevertheless been pursued with extraordinary stridency, even after the Reagan Administration had gone out of its way to emphasize the priority it attached to
Peking. No President could have conceded more than Reagan did in
the August 1982 communiqué. Nevertheless, the Chinese assault on
him inexplicably continued for many months. The ambiguous rapprochement with Moscow as well almost surely grows out of some in-

ternal maneuvering in the People's Republic — perhaps an insistence by the armed forces on some diplomatic respite so long as the Chinese military buildup receives such a low domestic priority.

Whatever the cause, US–Chinese relations are less good than they should be, given the enduring parallel interests of the two countries in maintaining the global balance of power. A stock-taking on both sides is overdue.

The real story of Secretary Shultz's visit to China will not be the familiar issues, such as Taiwan, trade, or normalization. At stake will be something intangible: the way the United States and China view their respective roles in world affairs and, above all, whether these views can be harmonized. And this trip is of enormous importance. It is crucial above all to be clear about what can*not* be accomplished and should *not* be attempted.

The Shultz visit can*not* finally resolve the Taiwan issues. In the Shanghai Communiqué of 1972, the accord on normalization of 1979, and even more explicitly in the Communiqué of 1982, the United States has repeatedly committed itself to the proposition that there is only one China and that it would not support any variety of a two-China solution. Moreover, the United States has already recognized Peking as the government of all of China. In the process, both sides have had to make painful adjustments on such issues as American arms sales.

The future of Taiwan must now be left to historical processes, and for the Chinese on both sides of the Taiwan straits to work out in their own subtle ways as Chinese leaders themselves have affirmed. What remains for both sides is to live up to the letter and spirit of existing undertakings. The secretary will surely hear Chinese views as to what that spirit entails. But formal diplomacy has exhausted the subject; the legal framework cannot be stretched further.

Nor would the subject of trade by itself warrant a trip to Peking by the Secretary of State. To be sure, trade and technology will become increasingly important to China (the speed of its modernization will depend on it). Both sides have real complaints. Our tactics in the recent textile negotiations have been execrable. Chinese bureaucracy can be maddening for American investors and companies to deal with. We have been too slow in fulfilling promises on technology transfer. The Chinese have changed their economic plan repeatedly in recent years.

But at the heart of these issues — and the reason they fester — is the inadequate political priority that US–Chinese relations have received from both sides. Neither country can want to — nor afford to — win these battles. Both have a stake in overcoming bureaucratic inertia and suspiciousness. It is high time for the top leaders of both countries to address once again the fundamental dimensions of the relationship and to lift discussions to the strategic plane.

Above all, the United States should show no nervousness over Sino-Soviet negotiations. A mature relationship between the United States and China can only be based on the premise that each side is quite able to assess its own national interest without outside instruction. Washington and Peking regulate their relationships with other countries not as a favor to each other but to serve their interests in peace, security, and progress.

If each side is wise, it will not deliberately jangle the nerves of the other by invoking a Soviet option. China is entitled to ease tensions with its northern neighbor if it can — just as we are trying to do — but it must avoid doing so in a way that makes Moscow the arbiter of both European-American and Sino-American relationships. Each side's freedom of action is in the end restricted by a set of truths that each ignores at its peril:

First, it is a preeminent strategic interest of the United States to prevent Soviet domination of the Eurasian landmass — the much-stressed hegemony — for that would shift the global balance of resources and power irreversibly to Moscow's advantage. A threat to the security of China would undermine the global equilibrium as surely as Soviet domination of Europe. And a weakening of America would jeopardize the security of China. Statesmen can make use of these facts; they cannot uninvent them.

Second, China realizes — even when it does not avow — that its frontier of over 4,000 miles with the Soviet Union is its fundamental security problem. As China modernizes, it turns into a potential long-range danger for Moscow, if only because it will be less and less subject to intimidation. Peking knows very well, moreover, that it is being wooed because the United States is in play; in our absence it might be threatened. Just as the United States — if it is rational — cannot push US–Soviet détente to the point of endangering Chinese security, so China, if it is farsighted, cannot wish to forfeit America's vital interest in its security and territorial integrity.

Still, reality is not self-implementing. In America, each new administration proudly proclaims the failure of its predecessor and its determination to start afresh — oblivious to the fact that this must unsettle all leaders who have staked their country's fate on the previous dispensation. The Chinese approach is patient and aloof; the Middle Kingdom has a horror of appearing as a supplicant. Washington acts as if good faith and bonhomie supply the lubricant of international relations. Peking assumes that its interlocutor has done his homework and will understand subtle indirections; the Chinese approach can therefore appear impersonal, even condescending. To the Chinese, Americans often appear unstable and slightly frivolous. To Americans, Chinese occasionally present themselves as either inscrutable or uncommunicative.

Thus both countries need to understand each other's psychology better and to establish the confidence that this understanding will last. We have to face the fact that the Chinese have developed serious doubts about our political or even emotional stability. At one point we seemed to invite military cooperation and then backed away. We promised cooperation on transfer of technology and in effect reneged. All this raised doubts whether we were really interested in a close relationship. Even when Peking acknowledges our commitment to maintain the balance of power, doubts have developed whether we are able to interpret it correctly in concrete circumstances or act on our interpretation.

When the United States is perceived in Peking as an inadequate guardian of the equilibrium, as it was over Angola, Ethiopia, Afghanistan, and Iran, there are two consequences: Peking is tempted toward Moscow despite all its suspicions, if only to gain time. And the bilateral issues of Sino-American diplomacy — like Taiwan or trade — must carry a disproportionate burden of the relationship.

Chinese policy and rhetoric of the past few years have made their own contribution to the impasse. It does not build confidence to urge the United States into a defense of the balance of power and then give it equal billing as a threat to peace with the Soviet "hege-monist." In recent years the vocabulary of criticism from Peking has been far more prevalent than that of cooperation. Peking must understand that only a relationship built on some strategic understandings and cooperation on some international issues will command American public and Congressional support for the long term. We cannot sustain indefinitely a relationship that in the public mind consists of constant irritation over Taiwan, some economic links (perceived as helping China more than us), and rhetorical battles in international forums.

Secretary Shultz — I am certain — will seek to make clear that we view the world in geopolitical terms relevant to Chinese perceptions. There are several areas in which Chinese and American views should be harmonized, or at least the range of our disagreements understood. First, of course, is policy toward the Soviet Union in general. In addition, we should maintain a continuing intimate dialogue on specific international issues:

• Where United States and Chinese interests converge and what may be done to concert our actions — for example, Afghanistan and Indochina.

• Where we have divergent policies but seek to avoid conflict — for example, in Korea, where we back opposing sides within the context of a shared interest in avoidance of war in the peninsula.

• Where we have different perceptions — such as the Middle East and Africa — but where policies should at a minimum not obstruct efforts for peace.

• Where on the whole American and Chinese interests run parallel — relations with Europe and Japan.

Of the operational matters, the only issue requiring urgent attention is transfer of technology. Our restrictions on trade with Communist countries have as their purpose to prevent the strengthening of strategic capabilities hostile to us. But China is decidedly not a Soviet ally, nor is it in the same class of military power. China could not represent a *military* threat to American interests for the rest of this century, by which time current technology will be superseded. China, in my view, should be given the same status for technological transfer as India and Yugoslavia. It would convey that we understand, and take seriously, the strategic parallelism of interest.

In my experience, the best approach in discussions with Chinese leaders is complete frankness. It is wiser to admit that some positions are in a state of evolution than to pretend to settled views that dialogue will reveal as shallow or empty. It would help if — as the dialogue develops — the American positions could be given as much of a bipartisan cast as possible.

At the same time, Secretary Shultz's hosts must not place the entire weight of the trip on him. It is to be hoped that the Chinese contribution will transcend the occasional hectoring of recent years, especially the grating tendency to treat American presentations as if we were students taking an examination. Peking has to assume some responsibility of its own for the balance of power.

I am convinced that both sides to this dialogue will be represented by men with the wisdom to transcend the recent past. Neither side can have promoted the visit in order for it to fail; each side knows that a failure would not leave us with the status quo but mark a setback. Nor can one single exchange provide the necessary depth and stability. Senior Chinese leaders should continue the process in Washington. And however difficult the dialogue may be, negotiating with the Chinese has the advantage that undertakings will be strictly honored.

Many American leaders have visited Peking in the past decade. All have been impressed by their hosts' thoughtfulness and meticulousness. None will have gone at a more propitious juncture than Secretary Shultz. I have every confidence that his trip will mark a major step forward to the benefit of our two countries and the peace of the world.

A NEW APPROACH TO ARMS CONTROL

Published in Time, *March 21, 1983*

THE NOMINATION of a new director of the Arms Control and Disarmament Agency has prompted a major Senate debate over whether the Administration is seriously committed to arms control. The controversy misses the real question: to what kind of arms control should the Administration commit itself?

So far, the controversy has focused on negotiations over deployment of medium-range missiles in Europe. But even a success in these negotiations — likely now that the German elections are over — will make only a marginal contribution to the stability of the US–Soviet strategic nuclear relationship. And here we are trapped in a conceptual crisis. For too long arms control and strategy have been proceeding on separate, increasingly incompatible tracks. Technology has driven weapons procurement at the same time that is has made irrelevant the traditional doctrines of arms control. Weapons systems and arms control schemes developed in isolation from each other had to be squeezed into a more or less arbitrary framework.

This article seeks to sketch an approach by which strategy and arms control can be reconciled and strategic stability achieved by ending the disproportion between warheads and launchers that is at the heart of the current strategic instability.

THE ORIGINS OF ARMS CONTROL

The concept of arms control evolved when a growing Soviet nuclear arsenal suddenly threw into doubt the comfortable premises of the decade after World War II. It had been complacently assumed that by means of the "balance of terror," technology supplied a shortcut to security. Even after we had lost our atomic monopoly, our superiority was so crushing that in 1954 Secretary of State John Foster Dulles could still declare a policy of massive retaliation, countering Soviet aggression anywhere by the threat to devastate the Soviet Union. There was little incentive to decide a question that seemed then only esoteric: what were rational targets for the apocalyptic arsenal we were assembling?

Soviet hydrogen weapons and Sputnik foreshadowed a kind of stalemate. Once general nuclear war threatened both sides with tens of millions of casualties, the very existence of nuclear arsenals came to be perceived by many as a menace. Traditional wars had been sustained by the conviction that the consequences of defeat or surrender were worse than the costs of resistance. The nuclear specter banished that conviction. Fewer and fewer objectives seemed worth the cost or the risk.

One result has been the growing determination to stabilize and ideally to reverse the arms race by negotiated agreement. There are at least two unprecedented aspects to the *nuclear* arms race. The destructiveness of the weaponry sets an upper limit beyond which additions to destructiveness become more and more marginal. At the same time, the complex technology of the nuclear age raises the danger of an automaticity that might elude rational control. For if one side should destroy the retaliatory force of its adversary, it would be in a position to impose its terms. That prospect could tempt the intended victim to undertake a "preemptive" first strike — or launch its weapons on warning. Mutual fear could turn a crisis into a catastrophe. Proponents of arms control thus saw it as their immediate objective to reduce the incentives and possibilities of surprise attack.

The goal was to reduce the vulnerability of strategic forces by maintaining symmetrical numbers of strategic weapons. If neither side could hope to destroy its opponent, the incentive for surprise attack would disappear in the face of certain and intolerable retribution. So long as missiles had single warheads and airplanes needed hours to reach their targets, a surprise attack would require a vast numerical preponderance. (Even with highly accurate missiles, an attacker probably would not risk a first strike without two warheads for each target, to allow for malfunctioning, hardened targets, or errors in accuracy.)

In these circumstances, numerically equal retaliatory forces were rightly conceived as adequate insurance against surprise attack. The optimum total should be large enough so that it could be overwhelmed only by a violation of the agreement too large to be hidden. Yet it should involve a ceiling that would stop the accumulation of strategic weapons. This was the intellectual basis of the arms limitation talks proposed by President Johnson and implemented by President Nixon.

During 1969 and 1970, the Nixon Administration undertook painstaking studies to determine the lowest level above which a strategically significant violation could not be concealed. The culmination was the SALT agreements of 1972. These accords severely limited antiballistic missile defenses to discourage an aggressor from believing he could launch a surprise attack and then defend against a counterblow. The agreements also froze the number of offensive missiles for five years. At that point the Soviets had a numerical edge in missiles — though not nearly enough for a surprise attack with single warheads. But this advantage was counterbalanced, first, by our very large — and growing — advantage in warheads, since only we possessed MIRVs (Multiple Independently Targetable Re-Entry Vehicles) and, second, by our insurmountable superiority both in numbers and in the technology of long-range bombers, on which there was no limitation.

The SALT agreements of 1972 might well have achieved the objective of strategic stability. But both domestic and technical factors caused the accords to become increasingly controversial. The Vietnam war and Watergate disintegrated the political consensus behind our defense and arms control policy just when technology was undermining its strategic premises. In the climate of collapsing confidence, groups usually associated with humane views came to advocate that the only way to keep our government from using nuclear weapons was to deprive it of all alternatives to a strategy geared solely to the destruction of the Soviet population; never mind that the targeting of civilians guaranteed mutual annihilation. The other end of the spectrum disdained the proposition that we lived in a new world. It insisted that arms control was a trap and a delusion.

As we consumed ourselves in disputes over negotiations and weapons systems, SALT I, at first widely acclaimed, was drawn into that vortex. SALT II never emerged from it. Advocates of arms control belittled the extent to which it was being overtaken by technology. Opponents focused on the numerical "advantage" that SALT I allegedly gave the Soviets, overlooking that the agreed totals reflected exactly the level of US forces the Pentagon chose long before there was any thought of arms control and that we retained a large numerical edge in warheads and airplanes.

Almost totally obscured in this debate was the reality that multiple warheads were making the traditional SALT approach obsolete. In SALT I a rough balance in the two sides' delivery vehicles substantially reduced the possibility of surprise attack. But multiple warheads — far exceeding the number of launchers — were bound to restore the advantage of the attacker, who could hope to overwhelm the opponent's fixed missile sites *even with equal numbers of missiles and warheads on both sides.* The side striking first would have an advantage — thus reviving the destabilizing danger of surprise attack. From this point of view, a "freeze" would perpetuate an inherently precarious state of affairs.

Fairness compels me to point out that the decision to proceed with MIRVs was taken by President Johnson and was made irrevocable in the Nixon Administration. We proceeded because in the climate of the Vietnam period we were reluctant to give up the one strategic offensive program that was funded with which to counter the rapid Soviet missile force buildup; because we doubted that the Soviets could achieve accuracies to threaten our missile force in the foreseeable future; and because the Soviets ignored our hints to open the subject of a MIRV ban in the SALT talks. Whatever our reasons, there can be no doubt that the age of MIRVs has doomed the SALT approach.

The controversy over whether arms control was a boon or a trap — and some ill-considered comments on the feasibility of nuclear war — left defense policy increasingly at the mercy of the exploding public concern about the dangers of nuclear war. No democratic leader can govern any longer without demonstrating his devotion to peace. The Reagan Administration soon learned that the assault on what it called the "fatally flawed" SALT II treaty made for better campaign rhetoric than foreign policy. It compromised on the strange course of observing but not ratifying SALT II. The Administration has proclaimed its devotion to arms control, and I accept its sincerity. The challenge it faces is to resolve, finally, the intellectual problem of how to ensure strategic stability amid the revolution wrought by thousands of warheads on only hundreds of launchers.

THE PRESENT DILEMMA

There is a "flaw" in SALT II, though not the one usually discussed. It is that SALT limitations were expressed in terms of numbers of delivery vehicles at the precise moment when the increase in the accuracy and numbers of warheads caused numerical "equivalence" to be more and more beside the point. With each side possessing the capability (the Soviets' actual, ours latent) of making its opponent vulnerable, arms control after a decade of negotiations had returned to its starting point.

This problem cannot be solved simply by deep reductions in delivery vehicles. Given the disproportion between warheads and launchers, reductions either are irrelevant to the danger of surprise attack or, perversely, *increase* it. With present weapons, the greater the reductions, the fewer would be the targets for a first strike and the greater would be its calculability.

This is well illustrated by President Reagan's Eureka College speech of May 9, 1982, which contains the basic American proposal for the Strategic Arms Reduction Talks (START). It was an advance over an uncontrolled arms race because it set a ceiling. It was an advance over SALT in relating the ceiling to warheads rather than launchers. And it stressed significant mutual reductions of strategic forces. It was a brave first attempt that unfortunately did not solve the root issue of multiple warheads. Even were the Soviets to accept our proposal, the Eureka scheme would at best maintain the existing balance; it would almost surely worsen rather than ease our dangers. A quick glance at the numbers involved illustrates the problem.

Under SALT II about 5,000 Soviet land-based warheads would be aimed at 1,054 American launchers — a ratio of less than 5 to 1. The Eureka proposal would reduce the permitted warheads to 2,500 on at most 400 launchers. Even were it technically feasible to distribute warheads in this manner (and the Soviets would have to redesign their entire strategic force to do so), this would give the side striking first an advantage in warheads to targets of better than 6 to 1. And at these lower numbers of launchers an attack would be far more calculable.

The Eureka proposal would also establish limits of 2,500 to 3,000 sea-based warheads. This would force a reduction of our submarine force from the 42 permitted under SALT to 15 or fewer (depending on the type). We could keep at most ten vessels at sea at one time, vs. the current 25 to 30. If there are any advances in antisubmarine warfare technology, as is probable, arms control will have increased the vulnerability of both our underwater *and* our land-based strategic forces — the supreme irony. The Soviet proposal of a flat 25 percent reduction in launchers, while simpler, suffers from the identical disability.

In short, a negotiation begun more than a decade ago to enhance stability and reduce vulnerability is in danger of achieving the opposite. Arms control is heading for an intellectual dead end.

WHERE DO WE GO FROM HERE?

We face two related tasks. First, arms control requires not so much a new proposal as a fresh concept. Second, it must become an organic part of defense policy. This requires that we return to first principles. The principal cause of instability with current weapons systems is the disproportion between warheads and launchers. All the remedies that have been tried are vulnerable to technology: hardening to accuracy, sea-based systems to advances in antisubmarine technology. There is no effective or intellectually adequate solution to this problem except to seek to eliminate multiple warheads within a fixed time, say ten years.

Fortunately technology, which creates the problem, can offer a solution. According to published literature, it is possible to develop a mobile missile that could be protected in a heavily armored canister. Its mobility alone could complicate the task of the attacker. Moreover, the new missile could — and should — be equipped with a single warhead. With strategic forces of such design, numerical limits would be both simple to establish and far more significant than under SALT II or START.

Once we decided on such an approach, we could proceed with it either as part of an arms control agreement or unilaterally as part of our defense policy. For example, we could propose to reduce and transform the strategic arsenals of both sides to a low number of single-warhead missiles over a ten-year period. The totals should be set at the lowest number that could be monitored, that is, at a level where a violation significant enough to overturn it could not be hidden. The permitted number of missiles may be as low as 500; at any rate, the number of warheads in this scheme would be only a small fraction of current totals, probably 20 percent or less of the Eureka scheme. Each side would be free to choose whether the permitted missiles would be mobile or in silos. Mobility would reduce the incentive of surprise attack, but equivalence at low numbers of single-warhead missiles would, in any event, assure considerable stability.

This course does not depend on Soviet agreement. It should be pursued whatever the Soviet reaction. If they refused our proposal — this one or another embodying the same concept — the United States could announce that after a certain date, say 1990 (or before then if the new missile could be developed earlier), it would deploy no more MIRVed land-based intercontinental missiles but would emphasize single-warhead launchers, the majority mobile. The size of that force would be geared to the number of warheads deployed by the Soviets; we would reserve the right to match each Soviet warhead with single-warhead missiles of our own. In practice, we would almost certainly choose a lower number that we calculate could survive the maximum Soviet attack capable of being launched. The purpose would be to increase the number of targets the Soviets would have to hit but without increasing our capacity for surprise attack. We would gradually phase out our MIRVed missiles. If the Soviets agreed to a formal proposal, schedules for the mutual destruction of MIRVs would be negotiated. If they refused, we would build up single-warhead missiles to a level consonant with our security. The Soviets could always put a ceiling on our deployment by cutting the number of their warheads.

This scheme should pose no insurmountable verification problems. Fixed launchers can be detected through national technical means; existing Soviet MIRVed ICBMs could not be made mobile; development of a new mobile MIRVed ICBM would require extensive testing, which could be detected and would therefore be proscribed. Mobile single-warhead missiles would be more difficult to detect; this is why agreed numbers would have to be sufficient so that they could be exceeded only by a violation our means of detection would not miss. Obviously, the more airtight the inspection, the smaller can be the numbers. Only missiles tested *solely* with single warheads would be permitted; any tested with a MIRV warhead would be proscribed.

No one can predict how the rigid Soviet bureaucracy would react to this approach. It may upset too many vested interests. The new leadership may be too dependent on military support to challenge its military-industrial complex. Yet sometimes an impasse can be broken only by a daring departure; surely the nitpicking SALT negotiations offer little hope for the traditional approach. If the Soviets can ever be interested in stability and in easing the economic burden of the arms race, they should — probably only on second thought — study this scheme with care. Like the Eureka approach, it requires them to redesign their forces; unlike the Eureka approach, it reduces their vulnerability. And upon reflection, the Soviets must realize that, one way or another, we will cure the vulnerability of our forces and in the process will almost surely enhance the vulnerability of theirs.

If the Soviets refuse to discuss such a proposal, one of three conclusions is inescapable: (a) their arms program aims for strategic superiority if not by design then by momentum; (b) they believe strategic edges can be translated into political advantages; (c) arms control to the Soviets is an aspect of political warfare whose aim is not reciprocal stability but unilateral advantage.

Where does this leave the MX? A Presidential commission is studying that question. I will address one issue: should we have a "counterforce" capability (an ability to strike accurately at Soviet missile silos or command centers), or should we continue to aim for "assured destruction" of civilian and industrial targets? Ever since the Soviets began to approach strategic parity, it should have been obvious that a strategy aiming at civilian destruction was an irrational, suicidal, indeed nihilistic course that no President could implement. Undiscriminating slaughter is not a defense policy but a prelude to unilateral disarmament.

Similarly, why should a Soviet counterforce capability — as now exists — be treated as consistent with strategic stability, while our attempt, represented by the MX, to provide a much smaller means to respond is considered as somehow destabilizing? If the United States, by its abdication, guarantees the invulnerability of Soviet missile forces while the Soviets keep ours exposed, any Soviet incentive for serious negotiation will vanish. A secure Soviet first-strike capability poses an unprecedented danger — ultimately that it may someday be used, in the near term that it may increase Soviet willingness to run risks in regional crises.

Whatever level of MX deployment is recommended by the Scowcroft Commission should be strategically meaningful beyond a mere token deployment. At the same time, the MX, like the new single-warhead missile, should be an organic part of an arms control strategy. To this end, we should offer to postpone MX deployment if the Soviets agree to destroy MIRVed SS-18s (their heavy missiles) over three years starting in 1986, and to abandon MX altogether once the SS-18s are dismantled.

This analysis has been confined to land-based missiles. Were the Soviets to show interest in the scheme outlined here, account would have to be taken of sea-based forces. Just as we cannot be asked to ratify our own vulnerability in land-based forces, the Soviets should not be expected to acquiesce in US submarine-launched missiles capable of surprise attack. Specifically, as part of the agreement proposed here, we should be prepared to move to single warheads at sea as well, though over a longer period, say fifteen years, because of the long lead times. In that case, the submarines would have to be made smaller and less expensive. It would be too risky to put so many eggs in one basket, as is the case with the current Trident submarines, each of which carries 24 missiles. A new regimen would be required as well for heavy bombers.

The deployment–arms control scheme would then look as follows:

A. The United States would make a fundamental decision to shift to single-warhead missiles as soon as possible. Ideally, this decision would be reflected in an agreed ceiling at a very low number — perhaps 500 — negotiated with the Soviets. An agreement should also limit throwweight to prevent development of huge single-warhead weapons.

B. If the Soviets refused such a scheme, we would proceed unilaterally toward our goal. The final size of a single-warhead force would depend on the number of warheads in the Soviet force and on what we need to assure our invulnerability.

C. The United States would begin deploying MXs starting in 1986. It would be prepared to postpone deployment if, before 1986, the Soviet Union agreed to a schedule by which its SS-18s would be destroyed over a three-year period starting in 1986.

D. Both sides would also agree to dismantle the remaining land-based MIRV forces starting in 1990.

E. In that case, both sides would agree not to increase the number of warheads on MIRVs while they remain in the force.

F. Other mixes are possible. For example, a small number of MIRVed missiles and bombers, no more than 200, could be joined with a reduced single-warhead deployment, say 300.

This approach would be a serious test of Soviet intentions. It would conclusively end the danger of a first strike. It would establish clear equivalence. It would transcend the SALT and START debate and put strategy and arms control in a coherent context. If refused, it would be a clear signal of a Soviet bid for superiority; we would draw the appropriate conclusions. If we proceeded unilaterally, nevertheless, it would be a major contribution to strategic stability and US security.

Of course, even the achievement of strategic stability would open up areas of concern now dormant. It would bring to the fore the pressing need to build up conventional forces to deter nonnuclear challenges. That problem would be addressed in a new environment. For all parties would know that they have taken — at last — a big step toward avoiding nuclear catastrophe. This is an imperative that humanity demands and reality imposes.

ISSUES BEFORE THE ATLANTIC ALLIANCE

*Address delivered at the Palais d'Egmont, Brussels,
Belgium, on January 13, 1984, to a Conference
on the Future of NATO and Global Security,
sponsored by the Center for Strategic
and International Studies (CSIS), Georgetown
University, Washington, D.C.*

THERE ARE two conventional ways of speaking about NATO. The first is to praise its achievements: the peace that has been maintained for thirty-five years; the cooperation between sixteen sovereign nations that has been sustained for longer than any modern alliance; the crises that have been overcome; and most recently the decision that NATO upheld to redress the nuclear balance in Europe.

Alternatively, it is also possible to deplore the unresolved issues: the gap between the announced military strategy and what is being implemented; the imbalance between détente and defense; the pace and direction of arms control; and the growing mistrust — nurtured by the Soviets — between a generation of Americans and Europeans who have lived their entire lives sheltered by the Alliance they assault.

Both interpretations offer elements of the truth. NATO is one of the most successful alliances in history. It has also increasingly maintained the appearance of unity by evading some fundamental issues. The newly elected Secretary General of NATO, Peter Carrington, walked the fine line between optimism and despair with elegance and wit in a seminal speech at the Institute of Strategic Studies in April 1983. He will no doubt lead NATO with vigor, intelligence, vision, and humanity; he is in fact one cause for optimism. I tend to be — let us be frank — somewhat apocalyptic. What I say hopefully reflects the spirit of his remarks; but freed of the responsibilities that inhere in a diplomat, I am more explicit about some of the unsolved problems of NATO as I see them.

There is no immediate crisis. Yet the demonstrations in the streets and the timidity of some governments bring home to us that there is no cause for complacency. Sooner or later a price must be paid for evading key problems — unless one is very lucky. And luck usually comes only to those who do not rely on it; luck, it has been said, is the residue of design.

In this spirit I shall deal with three issues:

- The perennial nuclear problem — especially the growing trend toward the no-first-use doctrine
- INF [Intermediate-range Nuclear Forces] negotiations
- East-West relations

THE STRATEGIC ISSUES — THE NO-FIRST-USE DOCTRINE

The dilemma posed by nuclear weapons has been repeated so often over the past three decades that it scarcely requires even a brief summary. In the late forties and fifties the leaders of the West thought they could compensate by the destructiveness of nuclear weapons for what they believed to be Soviet superiority in manpower. But nuclear weapons could fill the gap — real or postulated — only so long as leaders and public opinion were convinced that they had the capacity to reduce a Soviet counterblow to tolerable proportions, and even then only if a Western first strike would involve Soviet casualties compatible with our moral convictions.

These conditions began to evaporate in the sixties. Technology tended toward equality at least in the sense that a strategic exchange was certain to produce casualties on both sides such that any additional capacity to cause damage would lose all relationship to conceivable objectives.

That trend was accelerated by the Vietnam trauma. Western military budgets came under increasing public scrutiny and assault. Since the early seventies no strategic weapons system has been deployed in the United States without debilitating controversy and protracted delay. Parity became fashionable even before it became inevitable. Arms control theory and practice institutionalized it.

The premises of NATO strategy have thus been systematically eroded partly by choice, largely by inevitable trends. But NATO doctrine did not change. Lip service was paid to increased conventional defense; some increases in fact did take place though never enough to catch up with the massive Soviet rearmament effort. Flexible response based on the gradual though systematic escalation up the nuclear ladder has remained the NATO doctrine.

The result is the anomalous nature of the strategic debate. NATO's defense rests ultimately on nuclear weapons. Yet public uneasiness about nuclear war is growing; stirred to near irrationality by groups, some well-meaning, who believe that engendering panic is the best means of accomplishing their purpose of preventing nuclear conflict. Governments afraid to fight for their operational policies have compounded the confusion.

No leader of the West today dares to affirm what his strategy dictates: that to avoid defeat he would be obliged to resort to nuclear weapons. President Reagan and Secretary of Defense Caspar Weinberger were widely condemned in Europe when they referred to the "winnability" of nuclear war. The idea of "winning" a nuclear war was hardly felicitous. But the verbal formulation probed for an elemental truth: unless some rational military objective can be assigned to nuclear strategy, both leaders and publics will become increasingly demoralized by the still firmly enshrined NATO doctrine.

Since then both the President and his Cabinet have not only retreated; they have explicitly disavowed their claim that nuclear war is winnable. It is a tragic symptom of the gap in understanding between our Administration and its European critics that these fervent disavowals are disregarded and disbelieved; that most of our critics insist on holding President Reagan and Secretary Weinberger to their original declarations.

What political leaders hint, private citizens make explicit. In 1982 four distinguished Americans, all having held high office — Robert McNamara, Gerard Smith, McGeorge Bundy, and George Kennan — proposed the unilateral renunciation of the first use of nuclear weapons. Mr. McNamara reinforced that statement later by asserting that as Secretary of Defense in the early sixties and originator of the concept of flexible response, he had urged his Presidents never to use nuclear weapons under any circumstances. That view has since spread; public opinion is in fact tacitly sliding toward a no-first-use doctrine.

There can be no question that NATO should be in a position where it is not forced to resort to use nuclear weapons at an early stage of a conflict. Hopefully it will become strong enough so that it can repel any level of conventional attack by conventional means. The need to build up NATO's conventional capability has been passionately affirmed for a long time; for an equal period the target has proved elusive. The United States will not reintroduce the draft; its allies will give priority to domestic concerns over a serious defense buildup.

Thus it is one thing to advocate a strengthened conventional defense, as I have consistently done with many here. It is quite another to renounce the first use of nuclear weapons. If history teaches anything, it is that deterrence with conventional weapons is a chancy enterprise. Europeans have seen wars break out for hundreds of years between armies that were thought to be evenly matched. (Even at the outset of World War II the French army was considered to be — and in fact was — superior in numbers and equipment to the German army.) In conventional war, leadership, concentration of force, and tactics play a role which make comparative systems analysis calculations a hazardous guide to deterrence. It can be no accident that *all* wars in the postwar period have started where there were *no* American forces and *no* nuclear weapons; during that period Europe under American nuclear protection has enjoyed the longest period of peace in its history.

The tenuousness of conventional deterrence does not go to the heart of my concern over the spread of the "no-first-use" doctrine, however. For, paradoxically, the growing acceptance of the concept may well invite nuclear blackmail or even nuclear war. If the no-first-use doctrine makes any sense, it must mean that we and our allies would rather be defeated with conventional weapons than resort to nuclear weapons. But once the readiness to accept defeat is granted, why should it matter with what weapons it is accomplished? Why should one make the readiness to submit depend on the weapons used to impose an adversary's will? If an aggressor analyzes the implications of the no-first-use doctrine in this manner, he would have an incentive to warn that *any* war will quickly become nuclear. This would face the West with the choice of surrender or the kind of war of which our countries will then be incapable as a result of years of stigmatizing the weapons around which their defenses are built and with which our adversary's arsenal is replete.

But if we *are* prepared to use nuclear weapons rather than see Europe overrun, we are back to our original problem: the proper mix between conventional and nuclear forces and the appropriate strategy for the use of nuclear weapons albeit as a last resort. The question of how nuclear weapons should be used without destroying mankind remains unavoidable.

A rational treatment of this reality has yet to occur. Some experts — though declining in numbers and shell-shocked by the assault of the peace movement — still want to treat nuclear weapons as "conventional." This is clearly absurd. Another, larger group — ironically composed in its majority of individuals generally advocating humane and "progressive" domestic policies — have insisted that nuclear war must necessarily involve the deliberate extermination of civilians; they are convinced that governments can be kept from nuclear adventures only by committing them to the most gruesome strategy.

Politics and morality both demand that as long as nuclear weapons exist and nuclear war is at least conceivable, governments seek ways to limit their use and to terminate such a war *before* it turns into a world holocaust. In a world of tens of thousands of nuclear weapons, it is reckless to teach that any nuclear incident must automatically escalate into a cataclysm. If the worst happens — for whatever reason — governments have an obligation to humanity and to history to limit the consequences. Only nihilists or abstract ideologues can shirk that duty.

At the heart of the problem is that in nearly every country the consensus on defense and foreign policy has broken down. As a result, national security policy is too often overwhelmed by domestic politics. This could not happen but for two comforting illusions. Europe chooses to believe that in the end America will either prevent aggression or resist it with its ultimate weapons if it has no other choice. America chooses the illusion that with intensive consultations Europe will be induced to increase its defense contribution in the conventional field. Neither expectation is realistic — the European one slightly more so than the American.

If present trends continue, we run the risk that we are left with a precarious combination of the formal NATO doctrine of flexible response, which, however, now — unlike when it was first developed — has to be applied under conditions of nuclear stalemate, growing nuclear pacifism, and continued inadequacies in conventional forces. Left with no coherent defense policy we will ourselves have crippled our capacity for military response while sitting on the most destructive stockpile of weapons the world has seen and against an adversary whose political and economic system seems to have lost all vitality.

ARMS CONTROL AND INTERMEDIATE-RANGE WEAPONS

Not surprisingly, public bewilderment has turned into anxiety evoking an increasing clamor for agreements to end the arms race. Arms control is being asked to banish the danger of nuclear war and to reverse the trend in East-West relations. This places a greater burden on these negotiations than they can possibly carry; it is no accident that the Geneva negotiations have frozen at the precise moment that governments and public opinion in the West more fervently insist on them. Arms control is in danger of being transformed from a technical quest for strategic stability into a *deus ex machina*. Indeed, it is in danger of turning into a tool of Soviet political warfare — and both the West's strategic incoherence and its anxiety are principal contributors to that development.

The very idea of arms control is of course novel, if not revolutionary. Developed in its present form in the 1950s, it strove explicitly for stability by reducing the incentive for surprise attack not through arms but through agreement. The historically extraordinary notion emerged that a country's vulnerability was a strategic asset; with the civilian populations of both sides at risk, so the argument ran, neither side would dare to launch its weapons. Arms control theory contributed — in the West — to an aversion to defensive weapons such as the ABM; it also caused every offensive system to be subjected to extended scrutiny lest it somehow "destabilize" the military equation. Never before in history had military policy been judged by such criteria; but then of course never before had weapons posed such risks.

This is not the place for an analysis of arms control theory, which included many valuable insights. However, arms control, to be effective, requires an unusually delicate understanding of the elements of strategy. Nations have often suffered catastrophe in the past even when they fancied themselves superior; negotiating equality with an adversary calls for an unprecedentedly sophisticated analysis. The measurement of equality has been maddeningly complicated by the novelty of the weapons, by the asymmetry in the design of the weapons system of the two sides and in their geostrategic positions. Thus, even were the Soviets more ready for a serious study than they appear to be, negotiations would be difficult because the weapons of the two sides are designed by different criteria and serve different strategic ends.

The near chaos in Western strategic and political thought has magnified obstacles to arms control just when a definition of "progress" has grown elusive, and when Western governments consider progress in arms control a requirement of political survival.

The history of the INF negotiations illustrates these points. In response to the massive deployment of Soviet intermediate-range missiles, the United States in 1979 encouraged its NATO allies to invite it to station similar weapons in Europe. The vast majority of these intermediate-range missiles was in categories — such as cruise missiles — less threatening than their Soviet counterparts, which being all ballistic required much less time to reach European targets. But even in 1979 NATO did not dare to announce its decision in military terms, subject, as all deployments are, to *subsequent* arms control negotiations. The deployment became political with the so-called dual-track approach, which called for *prior* negotiations to ban the weapons altogether and make their ultimate deployment dependent on a *failure* of the negotiations.

The decision was fateful. Experience with arms control negotiations — or Soviet diplomatic practice — should have warned that an unambiguous outcome of such talks was nearly impossible. In its absence the deadline guaranteed a domestic crisis in almost all countries slated to receive missiles as the time for deployment approached. Indeed, it almost surely supplied an incentive for the Soviets to procrastinate in the negotiations to test the resolve of the Western governments.

More important, the NATO decision evoked a debate about the reasons for deploying the intermediate-range missiles — a debate which soon became bogged down either in domestic politics or in all the evasions and contradictions on the general NATO controversy. Opponents, appealing both to fears and to nationalism — especially in the Federal Republic — invented the argument that the intermediate-range missiles reflected our desire to confine a possible war to European territory. It was absurd. We already had thousands of short-range tactical weapons in Europe. Intermediate-range missiles added nothing to our capacity to devastate Europe; their distinguishing feature was, after all, the ability to reach beyond Europe into the Soviet Union.

The real justification for deployment was quite the opposite of what our critics alleged: to prevent the nuclear blackmail of Europe by linking the strategic defense of Europe with that of the United States. With intermediate-range American weapons in Europe the Soviets could not threaten Europe selectively; any nuclear attack and any successful conventional attack would trigger an American counterblow from European installations. The Soviets would have to calculate even in case of conventional attack that we would use our missiles before they were overrun. Hence the Soviets would have to attack the missiles if they used even conventional weapons in Europe; that in turn would trigger our strategic forces.

In that sense the American offer of intermediate-range missiles was a selfless act. If we needed intermediate-range weapons for purely *American* purposes at all — which is doubtful — we could have deployed them more easily and with much less controversy on ships.

Not surprisingly, the Soviets grasped the significance of the new deployment immediately; they had no difficulty understanding that a "linkage" was thereby established between the defenses of Europe and the strategic nuclear forces of the United States. The Soviet chief of staff, Ogarkov, has repeatedly warned us publicly that the use of European-based intermediate-range weapons would trigger an immediate Soviet retaliatory blow against the United States itself.

Instead of welcoming this linkage, which strengthened deterrence by facing the Soviets with risks they were almost surely unprepared to run, our European allies used it to press us to pursue the dual-track approach as an alternative to deployment. We in turn confused matters by putting forward the so-called zero option: the readiness to abandon our European deployment if the Soviets gave up their own intermediate-range missiles. In fact, the offer reflected a characteristic Washington compromise. It brought together three disparate groups: those who opposed the deployment of strategic weapons in Europe because they preferred a more purely American decision whether to initiate strategic nuclear war; those who were opposed to *any* agreement but supported the zero option convinced that the Soviet Union would never accept it; and lastly genuine devotees of arms control who considered *any* reduction, whatever its rationale, a step forward.

Had the Soviets snapped up the offer, or even made a counterproposal limiting the zero option to Europe, the United States would have been permanently barred from any *new* deployments. At the same time, the Soviet capacity to blackmail Europe would have remained unimpaired either through new tactical weapons or through the redundant warheads in their long-range strategic forces.

Symptomatic of the confusion in Allied strategic thought, many of our European allies interpreted our offer as intransigence. The Soviets having declared that they would never accept our offer, we were being urged to come up with a new position — that is, to abandon the zero option. In practice this meant being asked to propose an agreed, reduced level of weapons. For reasons of European internal politics, not strategic assessment, we were being pressed to reestablish the linkage between the nuclear defense of Europe and the United States which our offer had abandoned: to deploy some intermediate-range missiles in Europe; this time in the name of arms control.

The lack of clarity about strategic and political objectives continued to bedevil Allied policy. Yielding to Allied entreaties, we did abandon the zero option for an interim agreement on a reduced level of missiles for *both* sides. But no sooner had we accepted their advice than some European governments sought to mollify an increasingly restive public opinion by pressing for more concessions. This required lowering the proposed ceiling and indeed permitting some disparity in Moscow's favor. And when in effect we went along with that approach we were still being blamed for the deadlock. The intransigence of the Reagan Administration having achieved an almost folkloric character in European critical literature, the myth developed that the United States had missed a great opportunity by not following up sufficiently rapidly on results of the so-called "walk in the woods" between Soviet and American negotiators at Geneva in July 1982. On that occasion, US Ambassador Paul Nitze had proposed a ceiling of intermediate-range missiles on both sides and the abandonment of Pershing II missiles; the Soviets either had or had not — depending on whose version one heard — participated in drafting the document before agreeing to transmit it to Moscow.

This is not the occasion to analyze what actually occurred. It is undisputed that our decision-making process reacted to the Nitze formula in its usual cumbersome way — but then it had had no advance notice. This was neither surprising nor particularly significant. Nor does it sustain the charge of a missed opportunity. For the Soviets rejected the Nitze formula in September 1982 and did so again in October 1983, when they dismissed the latest American offer which was very close to the original Nitze concept. The sole difference in the current US proposal of a ceiling of 100 intermediate-range missiles is the retention of 36 Pershing IIs, a number not even the most paranoid Soviet leader could — given the thousands of Soviet warheads aimed at Europe — consider a threat of surprise attack.

The Soviets rejected the offer not because of the inclusion of the Pershings or the inadequacy of the ceiling, but because in the INF talks their strategy has been consistently offensive. Their objective has never wavered; they were bent on ejecting American intermediate-range missiles from Europe altogether — showing that they at least grasped the strategic and political issues involved. And all of this agitation occurred when the Soviets had already deployed more than 200 SS-20s in Europe and the first American missile had yet to arrive in Europe.

The Soviets understand very well from our current proposal — and many public statements — that the United States is willing to settle for a relatively small number of missiles stationed in Europe. Their argument about the shortened warning time caused by Pershing II is for the gullible. What decisive impact could 36 Pershings have? A Pershing takes eight to ten minutes to reach the Soviet Union from Western Europe. An ICBM takes twenty-five to thirty minutes from the United States; a submarine-launched missile, depending on its location, requires fifteen to twenty minutes. Were the Pershings to be removed what would the Soviets do with the extra few minutes of warning time? And since our offer does not require counting the SS-20s deployed in Asia, the Soviets have a numerical advantage even in Europe, for two-thirds of their Asian deployment can cover most of Europe. (I say this not as a criticism of our offer, for the essential element of our deployment is the linkage of the nuclear defense of Europe and the United States, which our offer retains.)

The Soviets again dismissed our proposal and walked out of the talks because contrary to the arguments of our critics and the ambivalence of many governments, they are at present conducting the negotiations as a political maneuver. They have so far refused to settle for less than expelling American intermediate-range missiles from Europe because they are striving for a larger objective than stability. It is nothing less than changing the political complexion of NATO.

If they were to succeed, for the second time in ten years, the Soviets would stop a NATO deployment to which governments had committed themselves for many years — the neutron bomb in 1978 and now the intermediate-range missiles. The practical effect would be to give the Soviet Union a veto over future NATO deployments — at least in the nuclear field. And the way would be open for the selective nuclear blackmail of Europe. After a brief period of relief the NATO countries would recognize the weakening of the American nuclear shield. This would be especially true in the non-member countries. They would realize their special danger; neutralism or a resentful kind of nationalism could develop. The Soviets would be close to achieving what they first proposed to the United States during the negotiations for the Agreement on the Prevention of Nuclear War in 1974: that in case of a European war the use of nuclear weapons be restricted to the countries of Europe excluding the Soviet Union and the United States. We rejected that proposal then. It would be ironic to create the objective conditions for it now in the guise of arms control.

The argument that the British and French forces can balance the Soviet SS-20s is either sophistry or a misunderstanding. Given the huge disparity in warheads between France and Great Britain on the one side and the Soviet Union on the other, it is self-evident that British and French nuclear forces can deter only a nuclear attack on these countries — if that. They can offer no protection to other NATO allies; they create no threat of a first use — whatever the extremity in which NATO conventional forces might find themselves. At some point, when the number of their warheads increases, the British and French forces should be included in the START talks. At present, unless linked to the American deterrent, they are nearly irrelevant to the defense of Europe.

The fundamental INF problem is quite simple. If the Soviets' objective is truly to prevent a surprise attack from our European deployments, an agreement on numbers and composition will be easy and rapid. What we should not do is to abandon the deployment of missiles in Europe altogether. And if the Soviets insist on that, it will be clear proof that their objective will be to wreck the Western Alliance. If our allies cannot bring themselves to say this clearly to their publics, they will only have themselves to blame when they are engulfed by creeping pacifism and neutralism. And in that case, the psychological basis for keeping the missiles in Europe will erode first in Europe but eventually also in the United States.

To be sure, it is highly desirable for the INF talks to resume. But the very plaintiveness of Western appeals gives the Soviets an incentive to continue on the political offensive. And if and when the talks resume, it is essential that the Western countries show more fortitude and unity than heretofore. The attitude of too many Allied governments toward deployment is like that of a host to an unwanted guest whose invitation to dinner it would be too embarrassing to withdraw. So long as there exists a nearly desperate longing for a negotiating gimmick, so long as the United States is automatically blamed for *any* impasse, Soviet intransigence is likely to be spurred by the hope that persistence in their present course will unravel the Alliance.

When and if negotiations start again, our allies, in the interest of the very progress they seek, should cease to demand new concessions before the Soviets have agreed even to the principle of equivalence. There have been three major and two minor adjustments in our INF position in one year, in large part to placate Allied public opinion. But when positions succeed each other at a dizzying pace none is understood any longer. Fuel is given to the argument that we are cynical, that we do not know what we are doing, that our basic position is flawed. The Soviets will have no incentive to change course if they perceive the Alliance engaged in competitive gimmickry. The United States has made its share of mistakes, but the root cause of the difficulty in INF negotiations is a Soviet assault on the existing political equilibrium in Europe.

There are many technical means to overcome the impasse. If the Soviets require a face-saving formula to renew talks, the START and INF talks could be merged — though I suspect it would prolong and complicate both sets of negotiations. It will not solve the root problem, however. Progress is not possible until the Soviets accept the principle that US intermediate-range missiles must be included in any agreed levels for the intermediate-range forces of both sides. Once that principle is accepted progress will be rapid.

EAST-WEST RELATIONS

In the public debate within the Alliance it has become nearly axiomatic that East-West relations have never been worse. Many Europeans profess to be convinced that American unpredictability and changeability have combined with confrontational and bellicose rhetoric to drive the Soviets into resentful hostility. Many Americans are of the opinion that European irresolution and domestic weakness encourage the Soviet assault on the postwar political balance in Europe.

As in all family quarrels there has been an element of truth on both sides.

Since the collapse of the postwar consensus during the Vietnam War, American policy *has* been extraordinarily changeable. The détente of the early 1970s was assaulted by an odd and unprecedented coalition of liberals and conservatives who could never have been united but for the collapse of Executive authority caused by Watergate. The liberals attacked détente for being too concerned with the balance of power while conservatives damned it for being insufficiently ideological or "moral." That coalition succeeded on the one hand in destroying both the incentives and the penalties on which détente was based; on the other hand, still in the thrall of the Vietnam trauma it was not prepared to face the consequences of renewed Soviet intransigence.

The critics of détente had a point when they indicated that the American public was unused to power politics; that there is no tradition in America for conducting relationships simultaneously cooperative and adversary. But that is precisely the challenge before our leaders. Any other course loses public and Allied support and enables the Soviets to capture the global yearning for peace — as the Reagan Administration has painfully learned.

The Carter Administration announced a "new approach" which criticized the Nixon and Ford Administrations for their alleged preoccupation with resisting communism. After at first rejecting the structure of SALT II inherited from the Ford Administration, the Carter team embraced it; but delayed so long that the invasion of Afghanistan defeated all prospects of ratification. The current Administration arrived in office rejecting the position of *all* its predecessors. It derided détente, refused to ratify SALT II even while observing its provisions, only to turn in the past year toward an obvious desire to improve East-West relations, even a summit.

The issue here is not what incarnation of American policy was right. Each was professed by reasonable people pursuing reasonable arguments. The trouble has been that each new administration has felt no responsibility to the legacy of its predecessor; indeed has prided itself on starting all over. Each reassessment of American policy left victims among European leaders who, trusting American representations and briefings, had committed themselves to the previous dispensation. Each reassessment shook confidence and encouraged European neutralism to become less dependent on our restless quest for novelty.

Nor has the United States been alone in changing its view. Our allies have changed with us though in a contrapuntal manner. When President Nixon came into office, he had a reputation as a hardliner. This triggered a succession of eminent European visitors to urge him into a rapid dialogue with Moscow — even though the invasion of Czechoslovakia was not yet a year old. A few years later some of the same Europeans warned against "excessive" détente. During the Carter Administration it was European leaders who first called attention to the need to counterbalance the Soviet buildup of SS-20s. And the Reagan Administration has become almost legendary if one reads the allegations of bellicosity, insensitivity, and major responsibility for the current East-West impasse.

And yet amazingly while it is easy to compile a record of ill-considered remarks of the Reagan Administration, it is difficult to point to much in the way of rash actions. Beyond muscular rhetoric the Reagan Administration has actually behaved with considerable restraint. What has it actually *done* to earn such opprobrium among our European critics? Why should intelligent leaders feel impelled to base internal politics on their ability to domesticate, as it were, the Reagan Administration? Why has the recent change of tone of the Reagan Administration — sometimes verging on the repentant — been largely ignored by critics and most Allied leaders? Is it because the critics seek an excuse for a barely disguised neutralism and the leaders require — or believe they require — at least the pretense of "moderating" American obtuseness and intransigence as a unifying element in their domestic politics?

European critics should remember that the wider the gulf between Europe and the United States the more difficult an East-West dialogue becomes. And the East-West dialogue urgently needs a fresh impetus. In a world of thousands of nuclear weapons the two sides cannot risk staring each other down or seeking to drown each other's proposals in invective or propaganda. The minimum requirement is that both sides understand each other's thought processes so that crises do not escalate by inadvertence.

For crises are almost inherent in the current structure of international politics. Both superpowers are associated with countries more concerned with their local rivalries than with the global equilibrium, much less with global peace. Our period should not be compared with the period preceding World War II when an aggressor launched himself into a quest for world domination — nuclear weapons are likely to inspire great hesitation, even among the reckless. Rather, the appropriate model is the period prior to World War I when client states pursuing regional rivalries drew their protectors into a holocaust by gradual increments, the full significance of which was not understood until it was too late. Which of the statesmen who entered war in 1914 thinking that the issue would be settled quickly would not have recoiled in horror had he had an inkling of the shape of the world in 1917?

Theoretically there are as well what the Soviets would call "objective reasons" for a constructive dialogue. The Soviet system is in trouble. It must deal with a leadership in transition, a decrepit economy, and restive allies. By any rational calculation the Soviet Union should seek a respite. It should know that a continuation of its present course runs a large risk of confrontation. Its leaders cannot be so encapsuled in their prejudices as to believe that they can defeat America without our noticing it sooner or later. The longer the process lasts, the more "successful," as it were, current Soviet strategy, the greater is the risk of some escalation. It is even possible that, whatever the current invective, Soviet leaders, when convinced that the current Administration is likely to be reelected, may well make some agreement by the summer. A reelected Administration, hence unconstrained, may be a prospect they would prefer to avoid.

But it is also possible that the Soviet leaders are under domestic pressures which prevent any policy adaptation or *any* farsighted policy for that matter. Before we yield to this proposition, however, we must test the possibilities of a dialogue systematically and persistently.

A number of principles ought to govern Western approaches.

1. Democracies have no reason to fear negotiations with a stagnant and brittle dictatorship. But neither should talk become an end in itself. The importance of a dialogue should therefore not be the subject of debate either within the countries of the Alliance or between them. The debate should concern the subjects appropriate to an East-West dialogue, not the fact of it.

2. There is need for calm in the domestic discourse of the various allies. There is a tendency to adjust the assessment of Soviet strength to preconceived notions of the Soviet Union rather than the other way around. The Soviets are neither as powerful or cunning as the opponents of détente claimed; nor are they as close to disintegration as some self-proclaimed apostles of peace allege. History will not do our work for us; but neither will liturgical rhetoric.

3. If we want to avoid the East-West dialogue's dividing the Alliance or becoming an end in itself, the United States and its allies must agree on a long-term East-West strategy. This will have to include the whole gamut of East-West relations, including East-West trade in its opportunities as well as its perils.

4. For arms control cannot possibly carry the entire or even the principal burden of the East-West dialogue. If too much weight is put on arms control, it is more likely to expose the raw nuclear nerve of the Alliance than to resolve it. Were Moscow to make a *political* decision to settle for the presence of *some* American nuclear intermediate-range weapons in Western Europe the INF issue could be settled rapidly. As for START, I have stated elsewhere my conviction that we have not thought the problem through adequately — but at

least we have tried to think while the Soviets have engaged in sterile repetitions of shopworn slogans. Still, even if attitudes should change, it will lead to a prolonged technical haggle; the subject is simply too difficult to permit a rapid resolution. And the best foreseeable outcome would be primarily symbolic. Some twenty thousand strategic warheads are in the arsenals of both sides. Even were the Soviets to accept our proposal to cut this total in half, the remaining warheads would be more than sufficient for catastrophe.

In short, arms control separated from a political dialogue cannot end the current tensions or even significantly ease them. Indeed, if the quest for arms control becomes too frantic, it will turn into a weapon of Soviet political warfare. Or else it will become a safety valve which the Soviets turn off to increase Western nervousness and on to reduce the impact of a new act of aggression.

5. The urgent need is for a serious *political* dialogue at the highest levels. The so-called confidence-building measures so beloved by professional diplomats cannot advance us very far. The opening of consulates or cultural exchange programs — even the prenotification of maneuvers — have at best a peripheral significance. In my experience every real breakthrough occurred by way of principals or their key aides who then gave marching orders to subordinates.

The problem is how to define the highest level. A premature summit meeting would involve exorbitant risks — though Andropov's health almost surely excludes it in any event. Heads of state cannot talk freely at the summit; their constituencies are always with them mentally; sometimes they are even in the room. Summit meetings, moreover, leave little time for real discussion. There is an inevitable time limit imposed by the schedules of the principals; there is an unavoidable protocol; there is the time wasted on translation. The possibilities of a breakthrough are usually outweighed by the penalties of failure. When heads of state disagree, there is no appeal to a higher authority; they would hardly have reached their eminence without a strong ego; abandoning a firmly held position would run counter to psychological as well as political imperatives. Summits can put the finishing touches on agreements reached previously; they are not well suited to break the ice.

One way to avoid this dilemma would be for each side to designate a special representative enjoying the full confidence of its head of government and foreign minister. He should be authorized to conduct private, exploratory conversations on their behalf, preferably without publicity. Each of these special representatives should have access to the head of state of the other side. Both parties would commit themselves to a global review of their entire relationship. As soon as the conversation between the special representatives demonstrates hope for progress, preparations would begin for a summit meeting which would then approve a full-scale work program for coexistence. But the method is less important — there are several approaches possible — than a decision on the direction.

6. So far, attempts to discuss political problems systematically have been dismissed as "linkage" and linkage is supposed to be bad because it is alleged to be an obstacle to arms control. By now we should have learned that the opposite is true. Arms control separated from any political context, is likely to run into a dead end. The danger of war, after all, resides less in the existence of the weapons of mass destruction than in the minds of the men who are in a position to order their use. And such men will be driven by political conflicts, not systems analyses.

A serious dialogue must come to grips with how coexistence is to be defined. Abstract though this may sound, it is at the heart of the problem. No détente can be sustained if all it does is to give rise to a political offensive designed to unhinge the global balance of power. One can cite several Western failures of omission and commission. But no spurious objectivity, no effort to find both sides equally guilty can overlook the provocations that accelerated the hardening of American attitudes. The dispatch of proxy troops to Angola and Ethiopia; the revolutions in Aden and Afghanistan followed by the occupation of Afghanistan; the Vietnamese invasion of Cambodia; the encouragement of terrorist groups; the massive delivery of arms to Cuba and thence to Central America mark a foreign policy that at least since 1976 has missed no opportunity to undermine Western positions.

I say this not to sabotage hopes for a dialogue but to define its essence. The Soviet Union must decide whether it is a country or a cause. It must be willing to define security in terms other than the impotence of potential adversaries. Some ground rules for coexistence are essential. Once that bridge is crossed, opportunities for increased cooperation in trade and culture would be high on the agenda. And out of such an exchange, progress on arms control would flow naturally, almost inevitably.

7. Such a process requires the restoration of bipartisanship in the United States and an end to the constant "reassessments" that disquiet our friends and confuse when they do not embolden our adversaries. The national interest does not change every four or eight years; at some point it must be fixed in the public mind if we are not to become an element of instability through our endless quest for ever-new dispensations. And it is time for our European allies to abandon the charade that their principal foreign policy goal is to moderate an intransigent America — a role more appropriate for neutrals than for allies. Those committed to the proposition that the precondition for peace is to insist on the moral equivalence of the two superpowers are in fact tempting a continuation of tensions by abdicating their judgment. The same will be the impact of those who confuse foreign policy with the liturgical condemnation of our adversary. The Soviets are realists. Sentimentality on the left tempts them into aggression; sentimentality on the right tempts them to exploit domestic and Allied divisions.

8. Finally, we in the West must be prepared to face the fact that even with our best efforts a thaw in East-West relations may simply not be in the cards. It is possible that Andropov is too ill and his colleagues too preoccupied with succession issues to change their intransigent course. Perhaps the emergence of the secret police in leadership positions means that the Soviets are applying intelligence methods to the conduct of foreign policy. They may have come to the conclusion that a relentless political and psychological offensive will wear down the democracies and they may be far from discouraged when they study some Western pronouncements. Or perhaps the whole Soviet system is frozen in inertia.

If any of these hypotheses turns out to be accurate, we have no choice except to stand on our best proposals, thoughtfully devised. The West need not panic at a period of deadlock. Its economy for all its shortcomings is more vital; its governmental structure stabler; and its overall power greater. The Alliance can thus face a period of holding firm with confidence — provided it preserves its unity.

CONCLUSION

It has become ritualistic to speak of the need for Allied unity. It is indeed periodically reaffirmed. But it exhausts itself in tactical agreement. Too rarely — if ever — is there a real attempt to project a strategy for the rest of this century.

And yet that is the single most important problem before the Alliance. I do not believe the present structure of NATO lends itself easily to such an effort. And I do not have much confidence in "wise men" exercises. Still a way must be found to deal with the unsolved issues before us. Nothing is possible unless we reexamine strategic doctrine without blinking. An approach to arms control must logically parallel this effort. It will be time also to look at the question whether every NATO deployment decided a generation ago must be sacrosanct for all eternity. East-West relations in all their manifold aspects need a sense of direction. The Reagan Administration has in practice abandoned its confrontational style. Our allies need now to avoid using the past as an alibi to avoid difficult choices.

The process is overdue and since it depends on the members of a democratic Alliance it provides no excuse for failure. The greatest encouragement to Soviet foreign policy in the West is the lack of clarity of the Alliance about its purposes. But that problem, being self-made, can be undone by our own efforts. Since the democracies have this possibility, it is also their duty.

STATEMENT OF THE CHAIRMAN OF THE PRESIDENT'S NATIONAL BIPARTISAN COMMISSION ON CENTRAL AMERICA TO THE SENATE FOREIGN RELATIONS COMMITTEE

February 7, 1984

MR. CHAIRMAN [Charles Percy], my colleagues and I appreciate this opportunity to discuss with the Committee on Foreign Relations the work and the report of the National Bipartisan Commission on Central America.

I should first note, Mr. Chairman, that a distinguished member of this Committee, Senator Charles Mathias, contributed significantly to the deliberations of the Commission. He served along with Senators Pete Domenici, Daniel Inouye, and Lloyd Bentsen as senior counsellors to the Commission, as did Congressmen James Wright, Michael Barnes, William Broomfield, and Jack Kemp. Senator Mathias found time in his crowded schedule to attend many of our meetings. And he provided us with invariably wise counsel. But I do want to emphasize that neither Senator Mathias nor the other senior counsellors who gave us such valuable assistance bear any responsibility for the Commission's report. That responsibility rests solely with the twelve members of the Commission.

As you will recall, Mr. Chairman, it was the late Senator Henry Jackson who proposed the establishment of a bipartisan commission on Central America. He saw that the crisis confronting this country in that nearby region called for a national response, above party and above partisanship of any kind. As a man who devoted his life to the national welfare, he well knew that such a challenge demands a bipartisan policy. In his mind was the Marshall Plan, that historic example of how the Congress and the Executive can work together across party lines to safeguard the national interest and advance our nation's ideals.

In the spirit in which the Commission was conceived we have delivered to the President and the Congress a report reflecting a broad and truly bipartisan consensus on the basic issues for US policy in

Central America. We on the Commission were of diverse backgrounds and diverse political convictions. Among our members were liberals and conservatives, Democrats, Republicans, and Independents. But during more than five months of intensive labor we laid aside partisan considerations and party labels. Our report is the statement of an independent citizens group, animated in the best American tradition only by concern for the common welfare. It seeks to convey an objective account of what we found to be the realities of Central America and of what we believe should be done for the good of our neighbors there — and for the good of the United States.

Let me briefly state what this bipartisan, or perhaps better said nonpartisan, consensus embraces.

First, the Commission has determined unanimously that the United States has fundamental interests, including national security interests, at stake in Central America. We have concluded that these interests are in jeopardy because of an acute crisis in the region — a very real crisis demanding urgent action.

The region's grave situation has indigenous roots. These lie in a long history of the exploitation of the many by the few — in social injustice, maldistribution of national income, closed political systems and governmental oppression. We subscribed fully in the report to the statement of the Catholic Conference of Latin American Bishops in 1979 that there is a "contradiction of Christian existence" in the "growing gap between rich and poor."

But in our judgment Central America's predicament has been brought to a head by the confluence of Soviet-Cuban intervention and international economic recession. It is the first that threatens all efforts to achieve peace and progress in the region. It is the second that aggravates human suffering and makes the prospects for its alleviation so difficult.

The economies of Central America, highly dependent on the export of primary commodities and on interregional trade, have been devastated by world recession and local violence. Gross domestic product per capita has declined since the late 1970s by

- 35 percent in El Salvador
- 12 percent in Honduras

- 23 percent in Costa Rica
- 14 percent in Guatemala
- 38 percent in Nicaragua.

These are grave statistics. What they mean in human terms is massive unemployment, more hunger, and diminished hope that the fearful consequences of the region's grinding poverty can be overcome. Today one-third of all the people in Central America lack sufficient income to feed themselves at an adequate nutritional level.

But the Commission determined that a restoration of economic growth alone would not reach the roots of the Central American crisis. Fundamental social and political reforms must go forward in several countries if lasting solutions are to be achieved. Above all, it was clear to us after these months of intensive study that the overwhelming majority of Central Americans aspire to live in freedom — in democratic, pluralistic societies. Thus, the cornerstone of the program we propose is the commitment of all the nations of Central America to democratization — and a corresponding commitment by the United States to support and assist in that process. We can contribute substantially through expanded exchange programs, through the National Endowment for Democracy, by encouraging grass-roots organizations where democratic practices are learned, and, above all, by making free societies a central objective of every one of our development programs.

Injustice and poverty create the conditions in which subversion and insurgency can thrive. The Commission's report argues that more widespread economic opportunity is critically important to the region's future well-being. We have proposed a series of measures to support agricultural development, strengthen small business and the small farmer, promote cooperatives, and generally to broaden opportunities for those who until now have been kept on the margins of economic life. Reform will ultimately depend, of course, on the policies of the Central American governments themselves. But the United States can do much to encourage and reinforce movement in the right direction.

We also put forth an extensive list of proposals in response to the pressing needs of Central America's poor for basic education,

better health, and housing. These include measures to reduce dramatically the scourges of disease and malnutrition among children, to
eradicate malaria and dengue fever, to broaden literacy and primary
education, and to expand low-cost housing programs, particularly
through private-sector initiative. The United States in our judgment
should demonstrate an unmistakable commitment to the goal of a
better quality of life for Central America's poverty-stricken peoples.
By doing so we serve both our strategic and moral interests. Here, as
in the effort to advance democracy, those interests coincide.

Our report addresses the requirement for immediate action to
arrest the alarming decline in economic and social conditions in Central America. We recommend an increase now in US economic assistance of $400 million, as well as other measures to deal with the
short-term impact of the crisis. But the Commission recognized, as I
am sure this Committee does, that it will take many years to overcome
the legacies of social injustice and economic underdevelopment. We
have therefore emphasized the necessity for a long-term program,
solidly based on coherent and steady US policy — a lasting commitment by this country to the freedom and welfare of our neighbors in
Central America.

The Commission's program is ambitious, but by no means extreme or gargantuan. What we are recommending in tabling the figure of $8 billion for economic assistance over the next five fiscal years
is not much more than double what the United States is doing now.
This figure reflects a careful analysis of the region's external financ-
ing requirements and is based on what I would describe as rather op-
timistic assumptions. In terms of Central America's needs, it is a
moderate request, one designed to help these countries return by
1990 to where they were in 1978–1980 when per capita income was
growing at about 3 percent a year.

To give structure, consistency, and continuing direction to this
sustained effort the report proposes that authorities at a high level of
our government meet with Central American counterparts to negotiate the creation of the Central American Development Organization
(CADO). In our concept CADO would provide guidance and review
for the development programs — economic, political, and social —

of those Central American nations eligible to join by reason of commitment to internal reform and democracy, as well as to external non-intervention. We envisaged other democracies outside the region as prospective participants. It was our judgment that to be effective CADO should serve as a channel for significant external assistance to the region.

Mr. Chairman, the distinguished President of Costa Rica, Luis Alberto Monge, has characterized the report of the Bipartisan Commission on Central America as an "intervention against misery and against ignorance. . . ." Those words are heartening indeed to my colleagues and me. That was our intention: to call upon our government and our people to engage fully at the side of our Central American neighbors in the struggle against misery and ignorance.

For that effort to prosper, however, more than reform and resources will be required. There must be an end to the violence that racks Central America today. The killing must stop so that the building of better societies can go forward.

A fundamental conclusion we reached after months of careful study was that the various elements of the crisis — the economic, social, political, and security issues — form, as the report puts it, a seamless web. They cannot be separated. Each impacts one on the other. For example, lasting progress on the economic and social fronts requires peace. The pace of reform and economic expansion simply does not match that of insurgency. Guerrillas can destroy much faster than reformers can build. But on the other side, peace cannot be achieved unless there is tangible hope for escape from misery and oppression. Thus, the Commission has proposed a comprehensive program to deal with all these elements. We are gratified that the Administration has adopted that approach in announcing the forthcoming submission to the Congress of the "Central America Democracy, Peace and Development Initiative Act of 1984." It is our hope that the Congress too will find the concept of a comprehensive program in the national interest.

I believe the report makes clear that essentially two situations in Central America threaten the security of the region and thereby the interests of the United States. The first is in Nicaragua, where an unprecedented military buildup, an ideological commitment to the export of revolution, and military ties to the Soviets and Cubans weigh heavily on neighboring countries. Last year 15,000 tons of arms reached the Sandinista armed forces from abroad, including Soviet-built armored vehicles and other heavy armaments. There are now at least 25,000 regular troops and another 50,000 active reserves and militia in that country of no more than three million people. No less than 2,000 Cuban military advisers are in Nicaragua, and as the Commission found for itself on our visit to Managua, the Sandinista military establishment is closely tied into the Cuban-Soviet intelligence network.

Nicaragua's menacing military machine, the Soviet-Cuban connections, and active Sandinista support for insurgency and subversion in neighboring countries create fear in the region — and threaten it with arms races and general militarization.

To deal with these issues, the Commission's report proposes a vigorous negotiating effort directed toward including Nicaragua in a regional settlement designed to ensure lasting security guarantees for all the nations of Central America. Such a settlement would be squarely based on the principles contained in the 21-point proposal of the Contadora group. These would include nonintervention and respect for national sovereignty; an end to the arms traffic and other actions directed at subverting governments; the prohibition of foreign military forces, advisers, and bases; a substantial reduction in the size and armaments of military forces; and the commitment by all countries of the region to internal pluralism and free elections. I emphasize that this last point would apply to all the nations of Central America. My colleagues and I felt strongly that it would be unjustifiable to ask more in this context of El Salvador than of Nicaragua. And we believed that by calling for democratization as an important element of regional security, as the Contadora proposals do, we were identifying ourselves with the deepest aspirations of the peoples of Central America.

In framing these recommendations the Commission drew heavily on our consultations with the leaders of the Contadora countries. We had the opportunity to discuss the issues of negotiations and peace with the presidents and other high officials of Mexico, Venezuela, Panama, and Colombia — the four members of the group. Their efforts to construct a peaceful settlement constitute a most important initiative, one meriting the unstinting support of the United States. You will note, Mr. Chairman, that the Commission's report urges such support and endorses the Contadora process as "deserving the gratitude and encouragement of all the nations of the hemisphere."

El Salvador's tragic civil war is the second situation in which critical security concerns must be addressed. It was the Commission's judgment that a stable resolution of that bitter conflict consonant with the aspirations and well-being of the Salvadoran people must be based on the democratic process.

The Commission determined that proposals for what is commonly described as "power-sharing" did not meet that essential criterion. Dissolving the existing elected government and replacing it with a provisional regime in which the insurgents would have a major role seemed to us neither fair to the people of El Salvador nor workable in terms of reconciling the contending forces. As we saw it, the final outcome of such a scheme could well be Marxist-Leninist domination and the imposition of a government unwilling to rest its authority on the consent of the governed.

But our report does recognize the importance of bringing into the democratic process those elements of the guerrillas' political-military front prepared to participate and abide by the popular will. In addition, the report emphasizes the necessity to establish conditions in which all political movements, including those of the left, can compete freely and peacefully for the voters' favor.

Further, we concluded that the establishment of such conditions should properly be the subject of negotiations between the insurgents and the government. But we found that time constraints and the circumstances now prevailing in El Salvador make it unlikely that meaningful negotiations can be carried out before the national elections scheduled for March 25. The report therefore calls for these negotiations to take place once the new government is elected. The objective would be to enable all who so desired to take part fully and without fear in the subsequent legislative and municipal elections.

I cannot stress too strongly how much importance the Commission attached to vigorous diplomacy on the part of the United States, diplomacy carried out, as the report states, to achieve the broad objectives of

- stopping the war and the killing in El Salvador;
- creating conditions under which Nicaragua can take its place as a peaceful and democratic member of the Central American community; and
- opening the way for democratic development throughout the isthmus.

But it was also our conclusion, Mr. Chairman, that diplomacy and negotiations do not take place in a vacuum. We cannot escape the fact that the Cubans, Soviets, and Nicaraguan Sandinistas are engaged in a serious and substantial effort to promote Marxist-Leninist revolution in the region. The armed insurgents who serve their cause are unlikely to perceive negotiations as anything more than a tactical maneuver as long as they believe they can win power on the field of battle. Similarly the Sandinistas would have no apparent cause to redeem the promises of democracy and nonalignment they made to the OAS in 1979 unless significant incentives and pressures were present to move them in that direction.

The diplomatic effort then can complement but not substitute for the other actions necessary to an increased sense of security and rising prospects for political and economic progress in the region. As I previously suggested, Mr. Chairman, our report reflects the Commission's judgment that all the elements of the crisis must be addressed simultaneously. We found no shortcuts — no gimmicks, negotiating or otherwise — to produce quick solutions. Rather, it was the view of the Commission that to attempt to deal singly with any one aspect — diplomatic, economic, political, or security — would be a certain recipe for failure. Thus, as one element of a broad program, the report recommends increased military assistance under proper conditions to the governments of El Salvador and Honduras. That assistance will reinforce the diplomatic effort by helping to create the conditions under which peaceful settlements may be reached and the objective of a better life in freedom for all Central Americans successfully pursued.

Gonzalo Facio, the former foreign minister of Costa Rica and a man well known to members of this Committee, has said of our report that it sets forth "the form in which these political, economic, social, and military problems can be confronted today — problems which have been incubating for centuries and which are now being exploited by the Soviet Union and its Cuban satellite." I believe that statement summarizes very well what we of the Commission were trying to do.

To return to the question of consensus, Mr. Chairman, you are aware that members of the Commission attached six notes to our report offering individual views on certain of its aspects. Two concern the anti-Sandinista guerrillas — the so-called *contras* — and one, which I signed with two other Commissioners, supports conditionality as applied to military aid to El Salvador but asks that it not be interpreted in a way that would lead to a Marxist-Leninist victory in that country. Another note concerns the conviction of one member that the report should have stressed to a greater and more specific degree the need to facilitate Central American exports to the United States. The remaining notes strike me as more in the way of observations or amplifications than dissents. Altogether these views take up a little more than four pages of a report 132 pages long.

To provide a general perspective, I would like to cite the concluding paragraph of the Introduction to the report. It reads as follows:

> Because the Commission has 12 members, each with strong individual views, there obviously are many things in this report to which individual members would have assigned different weight, or which they would have interpreted somewhat differently or put differently. Such is the nature of commissions. But these differences were personal, not partisan. This report, on balance, does represent what all of us found to be a quite remarkable consensus, considering the often polarized and emotional nature of the debate that has surrounded Central America. Among ourselves, we found a much greater degree of consensus at the end of our odyssey than at the beginning. This in itself gives us hope that the nation, too, as it learns more about Central America, its crisis and its needs, will find its way to a united determination

to take and support the kind of measures that we believe are needed in the interests of the United States and of the hemisphere, and for the sake of the sorely beleaguered people of Central America.

Finally, Mr. Chairman, let me emphasize that in proposing this comprehensive program for US policy toward Central America the Commission does not promise success. There are many obstacles. The problems run very deep, and have, as Mr. Facio says, been incubating for centuries. But it is the firm conviction of the Commission that a failure on our part to make this difficult effort will later cost our nation dearly. The threat to the interests of the United States can only mount rapidly as turbulence and subversion in Central America spread. Time is short. Let us make that effort now.

A PLAN TO RESHAPE NATO

Extract from an article published in Time,
March 5, 1984

[The introductory section of this article contained the affirmation that the "Atlantic Alliance must remain the pivot of American policy" but also the expression of deep concern over controversies within NATO as "unprecedented and unsettling." This situation must be remedied by "some basic agreement on political aims that justify and give direction to the common defense." The introduction reviewed·four areas reflecting troublesome differences between the United States and its NATO allies: the absence of an agreed, credible strategy, though existing NATO doctrine has become outmoded; differences over the presence of US intermediate-range weapons in Europe and the related problem of defining "progress" in arms control negotiations; controversy over an appropriate Alliance posture toward the Soviet Union; and disputes over European and American objectives in relations with the Third World. The article continues:]

THE DIFFERENCES between the United States and Europe could be healthy if they led to compatible and constructive policies for the 1980s and 1990s. So far this has not happened. Mutual recriminations have created opportunities for Soviet political warfare even during this period of stagnation in the Kremlin leadership. The Politburo is obviously convinced that the West has become so paralyzed concerning nuclear weapons that there is no urgency about nuclear arms control; the Soviets can simply wait for a while to harvest the fruits of Western anxieties. By contrast, there may be concern in Moscow that NATO will move to close the gap in conventional forces; hence the willingness to resume the talks, moribund for ten years, about limiting conventional arms. Does this reflect a genuine interest in arms control, or is it a means to thwart the desperately needed Western conventional buildup by creating the same conditions by which public opinion was mobilized on the missile question? And what is one to make of the almost deferential pleas by all major NATO countries for the resumption of a dialogue that the Soviets have interrupted? Or of the upgrading of all major European delegations except the French to the Andropov funeral, compared with the Brezhnev rites fifteen months ago — especially as Andropov's rule was marked by the flagrant attempt to influence the German election, the walkout from arms control talks, and the shooting down of the Korean airliner, not to speak of Andropov's fifteen-year stewardship of the KGB?

Will the Soviets see Western pleas for dialogue as a demonstration of goodwill, or will they learn from the compulsion to demonstrate good intentions after months of harassment that intransigence pays because the West has weak nerves? Will we fail to relax tensions because the Soviets conclude that atmospherics can substitute for dealing with the real causes dividing the world? Europe is not moderating the United States, and the United States is not stiffening Europe's spine, as the folklore on each side would have it. More likely, each is in danger of paralyzing and demoralizing the other. Western disunity is perhaps the principal obstacle to progress in East-West negotiations.

This state of affairs has deeper causes than particular policies on either side. The present NATO structure is simply not working, either in defining the threat or in finding methods to meet it.

Existing arrangements are unbalanced. When one country dominates the Alliance on all major issues — when that one country chooses weapons and decides deployments, conducts the arms control negotiations, sets the tone for East-West diplomacy and creates the framework for relations with the Third World — little incentive remains for a serious joint effort to redefine the requirements of security or to coordinate foreign policies. Such joint efforts entail sacrifices and carry political costs. Leaders are not likely to make the sacrifice or pay the cost unless they feel responsible for the results.

An imbalance such as the one now existing cannot be corrected by "consultation," however meticulous. In the long run, consultation works only when those being consulted have a capacity for independent action. Then each side takes the other seriously, then each side knows that the other's consent has to be won. Otherwise consultation becomes "briefing." Agreement reflects not conviction but acquiescence for want of an alternative.

The present imbalance is not new. It has existed ever since World War II. But military dependence on another nation has a cumulative impact. When dependence no longer results from wartime destruction but from a policy choice, made under conditions of relative prosperity, it can breed guilt, self-hatred, and a compulsion to display *independence* of the United States wherever doing so is safe, especially with regard to some Third World issues and certain aspects of East-West relations.

The problem has become even more acute because the generation of leaders that built NATO has virtually disappeared. Those who governed Europe during the early postwar years were still psychologically of the era when Europe bestrode the world. Global thinking came naturally. European leaders assumed responsibility for their own security policies and gave it up only reluctantly because of special circumstances. But nearly forty years have passed since the end of World War II. The new leaders were reared in an era when the United States was preeminent; they find it politically convenient to delegate Europe's military defense to us. Too many seek to position themselves somewhere between the superpowers — the first step toward psychological neutralism. Thus Europe's schizophrenia: a fear that the United States might not be prepared to risk its own population on a nuclear defense of Europe, coupled with the anxiety that America might drag Europe into an unwanted conflict by clumsy handling of Third World issues or East-West relations.

The rush to condemn our actions in Grenada by so many of our European allies is a case in point. What could have been in the minds of their leaders? Even making allowance — especially in the case of Britain — for totally inadequate consultation, they could hardly have wanted us to fail. That would surely have affected our willingness to run risks in defense of other areas, ultimately including even Europe.

Rather, they must have assumed that their actions were irrelevant and costless: that we would not be deterred, that we would exact no penalty and that therefore it was safe to use the incident to score points with "progressives" at home and with Third World radicals abroad.

The change in the nature of European leadership has been paralleled in the United States. Our new elites do not reject NATO any more than do their European counterparts. But for them, too, the Alliance is more a practical than an emotional necessity, more a military arrangement than a set of common political purposes.

On both sides of the Atlantic, we find ourselves threatened by the dominance of domestic politics over global political strategy. In Europe this leads in too many countries to a faintly disguised neutralism. In the United States it accelerates our already strong tendency toward unilateralism and isolationism.

US leaders have too often adjusted foreign policies to political pressures, bureaucratic infighting, or changing intellectual fashions. The history of the American attitude toward intermediate-range missiles in Europe is an example. These were proposed to the Europeans in 1957–1958, installed in Britain, Italy, and Turkey by 1960, and withdrawn in 1963. They reappeared later in 1963 as part of a NATO multilateral force, and were abandoned once again by 1965. They were put before NATO for the third time in 1978 and accepted once again in 1979. Not surprisingly, Europeans organizing to stop the current deployment are encouraged by the knowledge that previous American decisions have not proved immutable.

Similarly, our allies have had to adjust from passionate US advocacy of SALT II to its rejection, and then to the fact that we have chosen to observe a treaty we refuse to ratify; from a strategic doctrine of massive retaliation to one of flexible response; from a policy of détente to one of confrontation and back to conciliation, not to speak of the gyrations of our Middle East policy — all in addition to the reassessments that occur whenever a new Administration comes into office. Each change of course leaves victims among European leaders who have staked their domestic positions on policies that the United States later abandons. Each lurch encourages a kind of neutralism, as Europeans seek to avoid being made hostage to sudden swings in American policy.

A continuation of existing trends is bound to lead to the demoralization of the Western Alliance. An explicit act of statesmanship is needed to give new meaning to Western unity and a new vitality to NATO. In my view such an effort must have three components: (a) a more significant role for Europe within NATO; (b) a reform of the NATO organization; and (c) a reassessment of current NATO deployment.

A NEW ROLE FOR EUROPE

During the entire post–World War II period it has been an axiom of American policy that for all the temporary irritation it might cause us, a strong, united Europe was an essential component of the Atlantic partnership. We have applied that principle with dedication and imagination, insofar as it depended on American actions, in all areas except security. With respect to defense, the United States has been indifferent at best — at least since the failure of the European Defense Community — to any sort of Europeanization. Many in this country seemed to fear that a militarily unified Europe might give less emphasis to transatlantic relations or might botch its defense effort and thus weaken the common security. The opposite is almost certainly the case.

In the economic field, integration was bound to lead to transatlantic competition, even to some discrimination. What defines a Common Market, after all, is that its external barriers are higher than its internal ones. In the field of defense, by contrast, increased European responsibility and unity would promote closer cooperation with the United States. A Europe analyzing its security needs in a responsible manner would be bound to find association with the United States essential. Greater unity in defense would also hope to overcome the logistical nightmare caused by the attempt of every European nation to stretch already inadequate defense efforts across the whole panoply of weapons. For example, there are at least five kinds of battle tanks within NATO, different types of artillery, and different standards for calculating the rate of consuming ammunition. In a major conflict it would be nearly impossible to keep this hodgepodge of forces supplied.

Thus the paradox: the vitality of the Atlantic Alliance requires Europe to develop greater identity and coherence in the field of defense. I am not talking about traditional "burden sharing," paying more for the existing effort. I have in mind something more structural — a more rational balance of responsibilities. The present allocation of responsibilities fails to bring the allies to reflect naturally about either security or political objectives. Everyone has been afraid to take the initiative in changing the present arrangement, lest doing so unravel the whole enterprise. But since drift will surely lead to unraveling — if more imperceptibly — statesmanship impels a new approach.

STRUCTURAL REFORM

Structural reform cannot substitute for a sense of purpose and clear doctrine. But if pursued with care and sensitivity, it can help catalyze the development of shared political purposes. These common objectives require that European judgments on security, East-West diplomacy, and other matters emerge from Europe's own analysis. Mere acquiescence in American decisions, briefings, and pressures provides a facade of unity; shared purposes require a deeper sense of participation. Specifically:

1. By 1990 Europe should assume the major responsibility for conventional ground defense. This is well within the capability of a group of countries with nearly one and one-half times the population and twice the GNP of the Soviet Union. The Soviets, moreover, have to divide their forces on at least two fronts.

2. This requires that planning for Europe's defense become a more explicitly European task. Heretofore, the Supreme Allied Commander Europe (SACEUR) has been American. In the new arrangement a European officer should take that traditionally American place, probably with a US deputy. Such a change is also likely to give

a new perspective to Allied strategic planning. The United States has generally achieved its military successes by the weight of the equipment that our vast industrial potential has made available. This has tended to tempt our military leaders to equate strategy with logistics. European nations have rarely enjoyed such a material margin; rather, they have had to rely on superior leadership, training, initiative, and tactics — precisely what NATO needs in an age of nuclear parity and renewed emphasis on conventional defense.

3. Since the beginning of NATO, the Secretary General, who is responsible for running the Alliance's political machinery, has been European. In the new structure, with its greater emphasis on political coordination, it would make more sense for this official to be American — whenever the new Secretary General, Lord Carrington, decides to retire. Meantime, no Western leader is better qualified for guiding NATO's transition than the wise and thoughtful Carrington.

4. Europe should take over those arms control negotiations that deal with weapons stationed on European soil. The INF negotiations with the Soviets (for intermediate-range missiles) and the MBFR negotiations (on conventional forces) have heretofore been conducted by American delegations. Both of these negotiations should be "Europeanized" as quickly as possible, with a European chairman, an American deputy, and a mixed, though predominantly European, delegation.

The structure that I am proposing would enable Europeans to confront — on their own initiative and in their own context — issues that have been evaded for at least two decades; the precise definition of an adequate conventional defense; the nature of the so-called nuclear threshold — the point where there is no choice except conventional defeat or nuclear escalation; the relationship between strategy and arms control. Since nuclear weapons would presumably be used only if conventional defense failed, Europe would be responsible for setting the nuclear threshold by its own efforts; it could relieve its nuclear anxieties by the simple expedient of augmenting its conventional defenses.

By the same token, European leadership in the MBFR and the INF negotiations would place final responsibility for both conventional force levels and intermediate-range missile deployment in Europe with the leaders whose countries will have to bear the brunt — for good or ill — of the outcome of these negotiations. This is especially important with respect to the American intermediate-range missiles in Europe. That deployment makes sense only if the allies genuinely believe that the prospect of a nuclear blow from Europe on Soviet territory will help deter a Soviet conventional attack on nuclear blackmail. If our principal allies do not share this conviction, the psychological basis for the deployment will evaporate.

European chairmanship of the INF talks would oblige Europe's leaders to face the issue head-on; their domestic critics would no longer be able to argue (as they do now) that US intransigence is the principal obstacle to arms control.

As for the United States, it would of course participate in these deliberations — in a less dominant position — through its continued membership in the integrated command, its responsibility for nuclear defense, and its ground, naval, and air forces in Europe.

REDEPLOYMENT

The issue of redeploying American forces touches raw European nerves as no other does. The slightest hint of altering present arrangements jangles sensibilities; it evokes fears of American withdrawal and prospects of European neutralism. But if present trends continue, it is certain to become a central issue in the Alliance relationship. Before dealing with it in the context of a program of NATO reform, a few facts must be noted:

• The present NATO deployment of five American divisions and supporting air and naval forces evolved in the 1950s, when NATO's doctrine was massive retaliation — to react to aggression with an immediate and overwhelming nuclear blow against Soviet territory. Massive retaliation paradoxically required that the total forces on the Continent be kept below the level required for conventional defense. NATO did not wish to tempt Soviet conventional aggression by doing anything to suggest that a Western response would be limited to non-nuclear means. Hence the American conventional deployment in Europe reflected political, not military, criteria: it was intended to give us no choice about nuclear retaliation and to leave the Soviets no doubt that this would be the consequence of even a conventional war. European conventional forces represented a similar political decision: they too were conceived as a trip wire for our nuclear riposte. From the birth of NATO a full conventional defense has been part neither of its strategy nor of its efforts.

• This situation became anomalous when the growth of Soviet strategic forces deprived general nuclear war of much of its credibility. Yet NATO deployment has been essentially unaffected by the change. NATO has improved its conventional defenses but has not closed the gap in such forces. As the current NATO commander made clear recently, even counting the five American divisions that have remained in Europe, the Alliance is still unprepared to withstand a major Soviet ground attack for more than a few days. European ambivalence continues thirty-five years after NATO's creation. Our allies remain unwilling to develop forces strong enough to provide an alternative to nuclear weapons — and yet much of their public opinion shies away from even thinking about nuclear deterrence.

• Were we to start all over again, we would therefore hardly repeat the decision of the 1950s in today's circumstances. Let us assume a group of wise men and women from both sides of the Atlantic came together to plan a global strategy unconstrained by the past. Assume further that it started from the premise that ultimately the defense of the West is indivisible and that European security should be viewed under the aspect of the defense of the West in Europe — as a thoughtful French observer, François de Rose, put it. Such a group would almost surely conclude that the sensible division of responsibilities would be for Europe, with economic resources and manpower exceeding those of the Soviet Union, to concentrate on the conventional defense of the Continent. To maintain the global balance of power — by definition as essential for Europe as for America — the United States would emphasize highly mobile conventional forces capable of backing up Europe and contributing to the defense of, for example, the Middle East, Asia, or the Western hemisphere.

Such a division of responsibilities would also enable our military establishment to shift some of its intellectual energies and scientific research from a hypothetical esoteric war in an area where we have major allies to the defense of regions where conflict is much more likely. In such regions our allies are less prone to see their interests immediately engaged, and the countries being threatened are in a worse position to assist in the defense effort.

Even if we were to start all over again, an irrefutable case would exist for maintaining considerable American ground forces in Europe. This would be essential to keep our allies from feeling abandoned and to eliminate any Soviet misunderstanding that the defense of Europe no longer reflects a vital American interest. In a new division of responsibilities we should also preserve and preferably strengthen existing US land-based air power on the Continent. And we should continue our responsibility for both strategic and tactical nuclear defense, assuming that we and the Europeans could agree on a strategy for the latter. American intermediate-range missiles should remain in Europe to "couple" the nuclear defenses of both sides of the Atlantic so long as European leaders desired them. No change in naval deployments would be involved.

Why then is such a division of responsibilities not realized? The principal obstacle is psychological. For all their criticisms of American policy, Europeans dread a return to isolationism in the United States. Americans fear that any tinkering with deployment would drive Europe into explicit neutralism. And some in the Pentagon would rather maintain our troops in Europe in a less than rational deployment than return a portion to the United States, where they are more exposed to congressional budget cutters.

In my view, persisting in a deployment that is losing its rationale accelerates these attitudes. Pacifism and neutralism are on the march in Europe even under the present setup; isolationism in America is not yet so vocal but is being powerfully encouraged by endless allied disputes. An Alliance that cannot agree on its political premises cannot sustain itself by clinging to military arrangements decided a generation ago in totally different circumstances. With current trends the issue of the rationale for the NATO deployment will become unavoidable. If it arises not as an integral component in a comprehensive design but as a single question of whether to continue stationing American troops in Europe, unilateral changes will be arbitrarily imposed by the potentially most destructive means — the American budgetary process. Then indeed we might see in America a psychological wrench away from Europe and in Europe a panicky resentment against the United States. A change in deployment without a positive political and strategic purpose, withdrawal for its own sake, might shock our allies into neutralism; it could mislead our adversary and tempt aggression.

There is an urgent need for a serious and rapid reexamination of NATO doctrine, deployment, and policies, conducted by men and women known for their dedication to Western unity. The group — to be formed immediately after our elections — must begin with one of the most divisive issues before the Alliance: an agreement on the nature and scope of the threat. The group must avoid the tendency of previous such efforts, which set unrealistic goals and thereby magnified the problem. A deadline for completion should be set — certainly no longer than two years.

Theoretically, such a study could lead to one of three outcomes: (1) The group could come to the same conclusions about the optimum division of responsibilities in an agreed global strategy outlined above. Given the disagreements about the nature of the interests involved in regions outside of Europe and the domestic priorities of most European countries, such a conclusion, however rational, is extremely improbable. (2) The group could agree that the strategic interests of the West require a full conventional defense, but that for practical and psychological reasons, Europe can undertake the required effort only if the present American ground deployment in Europe is maintained intact. (3) The group could decide that the realities of European domestic politics preclude more than the current gradualistic, marginal improvement of defense efforts.

I hope very much that Europe would choose the second option. If Europe should agree to build a full conventional defense and were

prepared to express that commitment in unambiguous yearly obligations to increase its forces, the United States should accept the judgment that its present ground forces in Europe are an indispensable
component. Such a decision might in fact invigorate the conventional
arms reduction talks and in time lead to stability at a lower level. But
if Europe should opt for a perpetuation of the present ambivalence or
for only a token improvement, then the United States will owe it to
the overall requirements of global defense to draw certain conclusions. If Europe by its own decision condemns itself to permanent
conventional inferiority, we will have no choice but to opt for a deployment of US forces in Europe that makes strategic and political
sense. If nuclear weapons remain the ultimate deterrent to even conventional attack, a gradual withdrawal of a substantial portion, perhaps up to half, of our present ground forces would be a logical result.
To provide time for necessary adjustments, that withdrawal could be
extended over five years. To ease the transition further, we could, if
Europe agreed, keep the excess ground forces in Europe for a time
afterward in a new status analogous to that of the French forces, prepared for use in Europe but also available for use in emergencies outside it. Any withdrawal would make sense only if the redeployed
forces were added to our strategic reserve; if they were disbanded,
the effect would be to weaken the overall defense.

The proposed redeployment would leave intact air and naval
forces, as well as intermediate-range missiles, so long as Europe
wants them. A useful by-product of the process would be a systematic
reevaluation of the existing inventory of very short-range tactical nuclear weapons, a legacy of three decades of ad hoc decisions; these
weapons now represent at one and the same time an increment to deterrence and the greatest danger of unintended nuclear war because,
being deployed so far forward, they are unusually subject to the exi-
gencies of battle.

In this scheme, withdrawal would be not an end in itself — as it
will if frustrations on both sides of the Atlantic go much further —
but one component of an adaptation to new circumstances extending
over some eight years that rededicates the United States to the Alliance for the indefinite future.

Psychology is immensely important in international relations, especially when policies turn not only on cold, professional assessments of the national interest by trained political leaders, but on public opinion. I would like to believe that restructuring the Alliance to give Europeans greater responsibility for their own defense, while important American forces remain in Europe, will be seen not as an abandonment but as an embrace of Europe. It is a means of enlisting Europeans as full partners in the process of decision on which their safety as well as ours depends. For a son of Europe reared on the existing NATO orthodoxy, the very idea of even a partial redeployment is painful — all the more so after Lebanon. But we will not be fulfilling our obligations to the West if we fail to put forward an initiative to forestall the crisis that will otherwise confront us in much worse circumstances.

POLITICAL OBJECTIVES

By themselves, neither organization nor doctrinal adaptations can remedy the political incoherence rending NATO. This article has emphasized security issues. However, a few general observations on the Alliance's political problems are necessary.

• Those leaders on either side of the Atlantic who value the Alliance, with all its failings, as the ultimate guardian of Western freedom must seek urgently to end political disputes over East-West relations and North-South policy, especially Western conduct in the flash points of conflict in the Third World. The tendency to grandstand before domestic audiences, the growing self-righteousness, will in time make a mockery of the key assumption of the Atlantic Alliance: that we share a common approach to security. Defense requires, after all, *some* agreed political purpose in the name of which it is conducted. The Atlantic Alliance must urgently develop a grand strategy for East-West problems and Third World relations applicable for the rest of this century. Otherwise, it will tempt constant pressures and crises.

• The United States cannot lead the Alliance or even contribute to its cohesion if we do not restore bipartisanship to our foreign policy. Ever since the Vietnam war, we have disquieted our friends and confused, where we have not emboldened, our adversaries by periodic wide swings on essential elements of our policies. But the national interest does not change every four or eight years. At some point the national interest must be accepted by our public as clearly recognizable and constant. Otherwise, we shall become a source of dangerous instability, still relevant for our power but irrelevant for our ideas. A presidential election year is probably not an ideal time to forge a bipartisan consensus. But whoever wins the presidential election faces no more important and urgent challenge than to restore the element of bipartisanship to our foreign policy.

• European governments must meet head-on the disturbing trends toward pacifism and neutralism in their countries. These movements are led by people of conviction; they cannot be defused by accommodation. They can only be resisted with a compelling vision of a new future. If European governments continue to humor those who profess to see the danger to the peace in a bellicose America, not an intransigent Soviet Union, they will find themselves making concession after concession and will become hostages of their critics.

The current condition of the Alliance cries out for a rethinking of its structure, its doctrine, and its unifying purposes. The creativity and courage with which we approach this challenge will determine whether the Alliance enters a new and dynamic period or gradually withers.

I have outlined proposals to reinvigorate Allied cohesion by defining clear responsibilities for each side of the Atlantic, to be implemented over a period of years. On that basis European leaders could defend cooperation with the United States as something they sought as a matter of their own conviction and in their own national interest. American leaders would have a rational, understandable policy to defend and would benefit from dealing with a more equal partner. A new era of Allied creativity and American dedication could give inspiration to the generation that has come to maturity since World War II and since the postwar crises that infused NATO's founders with their sense of common purpose.

We must not let our future pass by default to the neutralists, pacifists, and neoisolationists who systematically seek to undermine all joint efforts. The nations bordering the North Atlantic need above all faith in themselves and the will to resist the siren calls of those who use fear and panic as instruments of policy or domestic debate. In the end we must fulfill our trust: to preserve and strengthen a North Atlantic Alliance that represents the hope of human dignity and decency in our world.

INTERNATIONAL ECONOMICS AND WORLD ORDER

Address on the occasion of the Tricentenary of The Mocatta Group, delivered in Washington, D.C., September 24, 1984

IT IS with great pleasure that I accepted the invitation to deliver the First Mocatta Lecture. It is not often that I find myself before a captive audience of economists and bankers — for reasons some of my former colleagues consider compelling. You should understand that I do not claim to be a technical expert on economics. My preocupation is with international order: what makes an international system function, the causes of its dislocation, and the possible remedies. My theme here is that the political and economic global systems are no longer congruent. As a result a number of countries sufficient to upset the equilibrium lack a consistent domestic discipline and pursue incompatible policies and the global economic system seems incapable of generating — indeed, it does not even attempt — a coherent strategy for overall growth.

The nineteenth century was a period of unprecedented economic growth which produced what we now call the "developed" world. The principal causes were a combination of technological breakthroughs and the compatibility between political and economic philosophies in the countries that shaped world affairs. Governments acted on the premise that the economic sphere was beyond its power or even competence. The accumulation of capital was left to the operation of the market. The mechanism of adjustment between economies was provided by the gold standard to which all major trading nations subscribed. All this had the advantage of automaticity. The market gave the signal when economic adjustment was needed; no additional political decision was required to trigger adjustment policies. Politicians could either accept the gold standard or reject it. But once that decision was made, they were forced to conform spending, taxing, and monetary policies to its discipline.

There were of course costs, sometimes heavy human costs. Severe unemployment and periodic deflation were considered "natural"; the business cycle was believed to follow laws beyond the capacity of governments to repeal or amend. International trade was dominated by a very few countries whose competition was more often governed by strategic than by economic criteria. Colonial empires provided the safety valve of assured markets and sources of raw material.

But this combination of gold, colonialism, and laissez-faire is not the current condition. In the nineteenth century the economic world order was established by a very few dominant countries which set the rules of the game, that is, of the market. Industrialization had been invented in Great Britain, which for a while had a near-monopoly on the relevant technology; free trade is easy to manage for the monopolist. The circle of industrialized countries gradually expanded (initially always behind tariff walls), but the economic system remained under the control of a small group of European countries with similar political systems and economies.

Even then the dominant countries did not adjust gracefully to the emergence of rivals. At the turn of the century Britain had trouble accommodating Germany. In the 1920s and 1930s, when rising Italy and Japan wanted "a piece" of the action, the failure of the economic system to accommodate them contributed importantly to rampant economic nationalism. In the fifties and sixties the United States became the balance wheel of the world economic order. Backed by the industrial democracies, it was strong enough to make and enforce international rules. This arrangement collapsed in the seventies under the twin blows of resurgent economic nationalism (including American) and the oil crisis.

The economic world order of the past cannot be resurrected and a new one cannot be created by the old players. Too many newcomers insist on participation. China, Brazil, India, Korea, in time Mexico and Indonesia, to name just a few, will insist on helping to reshape the rules which affect their economic and hence their political destiny.

The task of constructing a new international economic order is made more challenging because the most important economic powers are governed by a kind of popular democracy unknown in the nineteenth century. Suffrage is universal; the public insists that governments assume responsibility to alleviate suffering and to improve the quality of life, if necessary even at the cost of slowing economic growth. Few, if any, excuses are tolerated; the political landscape of the last ten years in Europe and in the United States is littered with the wreckage of governments that failed to produce economic results acceptable to the electorate — regardless of who was at fault. After the fall of the Shah triggered a new inflationary spiral, no national leader in office in a major democracy survived the next election.

For this reason alone the present international political environment is hostile to automatic mechanisms. Unlike their nineteenth-century counterparts office holders today are not willing to limit themselves to "on or off" decisions; they insist on controlling the economic policy levers directly in order to achieve immediate political goals.

This process puts a premium on short-term approaches; it encourages leaders to wait for crises to mature until action is unavoidable; simultaneously it tempts them to shift their economic problems to other countries for as long as possible.

The growing political nationalism runs counter to the dominant *economic* trends of this century. For the first time in history the world economy has become truly international. No geographic region is excluded from international commerce; each, with the possible exception of Africa, contains some major actor. But none is strong enough to impose its design. They compete through national decisions while being simultaneously linked by global markets. Not even the sharp political differences between the Soviet bloc and the West have proved an obstacle to these dominant trends. A conservative American administration has avidly encouraged Soviet grain purchases. Many European industrialists pursue in the less-developed economies of the Soviet bloc the opportunity or the mirage — depending on one's point of view — of a market sheltered from Japanese and US competition.

The incongruity between the internationalization of the world economy and the dogged strengthening of national autonomy in economic decision-making is the deepest cause of the gyrations of markets and exchange rates. Tax, spending, social employment, industrial, and trade policies are insulated behind national borders despite the fact that such decisions have global consequences in direct proportion to the economic importance of the country involved. A case in point is the unilateral decision by the United States in 1971 to suspend the convertibility of the dollar and to impose a 10 percent surcharge. The effect was to overthrow the Bretton Woods arrangement affecting all countries — without prior consultation or notice to anyone. Comparable unilateralism has marked the Japanese restrictions on foreign investment and Europe's management of agricultural policy.

We live with the paradox of a global economy which lacks a system for setting agreed long-range goals. Automatic mechanisms to force coordinated decisions have proved politically unacceptable. But the industrial democracies have recoiled as well from the alternative of political coordination of fiscal and monetary policies. Forums where national economic policymakers meet exist, of course: the Bank for International Settlements, the International Monetary Fund, and most dramatically the economic summits. But these occasions provide little more than an opportunity for an exchange of national views; they have not succeeded in shifting the framework of thinking and acting to a global perspective.

In recent years those charged with international monetary arrangements have tried to establish the International Monetary Fund as the global disciplinary force. The 1976 amendment of the fund's Articles of Agreements give the IMF the authority to "promote stability by fostering orderly underlying economic and financial conditions" as well as "to seek orderly economic growth with reasonable price stability." In theory at least this implies the right to review national economic policies for their international compatibility.

This "technicians' automaticity" works better in theory than in practice. The fund, though it may police a few troublesome cases, is far from being the governor of the general system. The United States and other major industrial democracies have been unwilling to modify their policies in response to IMF criticism. In fact the United States has been tacitly conceded a dominant role for the dollar and a disproportionate autonomy for its decisions. IMF discipline has in practice been applied primarily to those countries in economic trouble; most recently to developing countries facing a mounting burden of international debt.

In theory, of course, no mechanism such as the fund *or* a commodity such as gold should be necessary. The market should be an incorruptible judge of the appropriateness of economic policies. In practice, however, the dominance of the United States in economic affairs, the imperfections of financial markets, and the ability of countries to delay remedial adjustment through borrowing has meant that the market can be ignored at least for a while. To be sure the ultimate reckoning is all the more severe. But the temptation of governments to delay the bitter medicine of reform of economic policies — usually involving some contraction of nonaffordable expenditures — beyond their electoral period tends to be irresistible.

In these circumstances the economic system operates — if at all — as crisis management. The risk is, of course, that some day crisis management may be inadequate. The world will then face a disaster its lack of foresight has made inevitable.

The biggest politico-economic challenge to statesmen is to integrate national policies into a global perspective, to resolve the discordance between the international economy and the political system based on the nation state. The goal can be stated as simply as it is difficult to achieve: a dynamic and free global economy which will be sustained by key developed and developing countries because they have a stake in it.

In what follows I will discuss this challenge in relation to three issues: trade, exchange rates, and international debt.

TRADE POLICY AND INTERNATIONAL POLITICS

According to the maxims of the prevalent trade theory, the free exchange of goods and services potentially benefits everybody; tariffs and other trade barriers reward inefficiency, restrict commerce, and lower the overall standard of living. The professed objective of all trading nations is to remove political obstacles to trade and to rely on comparative advantage. But the gap between theory and practice is wide. Many nations, while paying lip service to free trade, systematically impede it in practice. Clearly important political realities are at work.

For one thing, Adam Smith and David Ricardo developed their theories when Britain had an effective monopoly on industrialization and a large advantage in the generation of energy based on coal. There is no doubt that free trade benefits a country which enjoys such a comparative advantage. Inefficient industries are replaced by more efficient ones *within* the same national borders; labor can move, at least theoretically, from one sector to another. Productivity, income, growth, and employment are certain to benefit — though the adjustment process in the nineteenth century was never as free of friction as the theory maintained. This state of affairs continued for a while after other European states industrialized. Cultural homogeneity prevented any country from achieving a unilateral advantage and colonial empires cushioned the shock of competition. Even with these safety valves the German-British trade rivalry contributed to the tensions that ultimately produced the First World War.

In our period, the number of actors has multiplied dramatically. There are more than twenty major trading nations, including the traditional industrial democracies and such significant exporters as Brazil, Korea, Singapore, and Hong Kong. The wage scales and cultural background of the major trading nations and exporters are dissimilar. With the best efforts to improve productivity, some nations — especially in Europe — will be unable to compete with substantially lower standards of living, at least in industries that are labor-intensive. Thus whole sectors of industry move from one country to another, indeed from one continent to another. This compounds the congenital unemployment produced by automation and rigid management-labor practices and generates pressures for protectionism.

The maxims by which the debt crisis is being combatted also tend to inhibit free trade. A key provision of every IMF adjustment program is to limit imports and to encourage exports. But by definition it is impossible for *every* nation to pursue such a strategy which is in effect mercantilistic. The limitation of imports must be at *somebody's* expense, especially if coupled with the systematic promotion of exports. And if the strategy works, developing nations are transferring real resources to the industrialized ones, the precise opposite of what is needed for global development.

Two results are probable. Either the quasi-mercantilistic structure will collapse because there is simply not enough demand to sustain the exports required by the developing world. Or these export surpluses will be sustained on a temporary basis by extremely unfavorable trade balances in a very few countries, especially by the United States. The US trade deficit is officially forecast to exceed $120 billion this year — a level unimaginable until very recently. Such a situation cannot possibly be maintained without causing our government to take some remedial, probably protectionist, steps which could collapse the whole fragile edifice of current international trade practices.

In short, free trade is being stifled by the same political factors which prevent automaticity as the adjustment mechanism of the economic system. The growing influence of domestic political considerations in all democratic countries threatens the open trading system as we have known it. Protectionism, trade restraint, and unfair trade policies are on the march.

A paradox follows from these considerations: for free trade to work, governments committed to it must to a degree retreat from complete laissez-faire. International rules are needed to avoid monopolies, restrict dumping, and inhibit export subsidies, predatory practices, and excessive uncertainties. National policies must ease the adjustment imposed by foreign competition and distribute the benefits of foreign trade equitably. Otherwise the system will not function; it will be overwhelmed by the political process.

To state these principles is to illustrate how far the national behavior of the major trading nations has strayed from them. The United States remains formally committed to free trade but it clearly lacks a coherent strategy to deal with the distortions caused by the protectionist and mercantilistic measures of other nations. Hence it is unable to insist on a coordinated policy. In practice our trade policy is a series of disconnected ad hoc decisions taken largely in response to the specific complaints of political interests most directly affected. These are by definition usually the least competitive sectors. So long as the impetus behind policy is the desire to localize the pain of a particular economic sector, the result can only by accident be the promotion of the common good of either the United States or of the world economy as a whole.

When theory and practice diverge, one or the other must give way. My strong preference would be for a firmly based system of liberal free trade. But this requires a major act of international statesmanship. Specifically, new and binding international rules need to be established to encourage direct foreign investment and to define codes of conduct for multinational corporations. These rules should apply as well to international trade in services and perhaps even to immigration. GATT must be revamped to bring it closer to the ideals of the International Trade Organization which was proposed by Bretton Woods but proved stillborn. It should be given greater authority to act against restraints on trade and investment as well as predatory trade practices. The newly industrialized nations, like Brazil or Mexico, should be drawn into more active participation.

But if such a policy proves unachievable, it would be foolhardy to pay lip service to a theory daily rejected by political attempts to maximize national advantage — in short, a mercantilistic world.

Japan seems to have come to this conclusion. It makes little pretense that its foreign economic policy is guided by a commitment to the free play of market forces. It is instead more or less explicitly geared to manipulate the trade system as it really operates to the national advantage. Japan is widely criticized for acting counter to existing economic theory. In fact, it is possible to argue that it is simply playing the de facto game more systematically and with greater coherence than anyone else.

But if we are driven to it we can play the same game, however reluctantly, and thereby enhance our competitive position in a world of unilateral trade practices and bilateral agreements. We need not fear such a world; its chief peril is if we fail to recognize its emergence. At some point the sheer weight of the United States's managing — in cooperation with like-minded countries — its foreign trade interests with determination and vision, will probably convince the rest of the world — to put it politely — of the need for more coordinated trade and economic policies. We would then have achieved a more coherent world trading system by the back door.

EXCHANGE RATES AND INTERNATIONAL COOPERATION

Ever since the United States unilaterally abandoned the Bretton Woods agreement in 1971, there has been a debate about the relative merit of a floating system as against fixed parities and at the margin even of the advantages of a return to the gold standard. I will not enter into the debate over the economic merit of the various schools of thought. The original argument that the floating system would automatically produce stability was falsified by the oil shocks. No exchange system could have produced stability when the price of oil quintupled within a two-year period. But even after the oil price leveled off, the floating system has not worked as smoothly as its proponents had predicted. Countries, it was held, would not accept an overvalued currency because it would reduce the competitiveness of exports or an undervalued one for fear of generating inflationary pressures. Hence, almost like the gold standard, the floating system was expected to force an adjustment of irresponsible or extravagant policies nearly automatically.

This has not happened because the impact of the market has been partially obscured by political decisions. In order to escape — at least for a while — the need to toughen internal economic policies, governments often ignored the market's warning signals and borrowed to finance current account deficits. And countries promoting their exports have avoided strenuous efforts to correct undervalued exchange rates.

In a sense, of course, exchange rates tend to reflect, not cause,

domestic economic conditions. Incompatible national economic policies inevitably lead to uneven development and crises which will be
reflected in the constant need for exchange-rate adjustments. The
United States is therefore surely right in arguing that correct economic policies are the irreducible precondition to exchange-rate stability. Confusion and growing resentment result, however, when the
United States insists that it is the sole judge of what is the right mix of
its own economic policies without regard to their impact on the rest of
the world.

The problem becomes more acute because we have the strength
to impose our views — at least for a while. The dominance of the
American economy explains why no matter what the value of the dollar we are criticized for its allegedly harmful impact on the world
economy. Five years ago at the IMF meeting in Yugoslavia the weakness of the dollar was the dominant theme. Today the strength of our
currency is blamed for our presumed policy to use the capital of the
rest of the world to finance the deficits which stimulate our economy.
In the seventies the "market" belatedly corrected the imbalance but
not until the Federal Reserve Bank pushed up interest rates. Today
these same high interest rates, coupled with the possibility of attrac-
tive capital appreciation and political stability, contribute to exorbitant exchange rates. The strength of the American economy is such
that whatever the value of the dollar the United States can take away
with one hand what it gives with the other. Today the growth in imports which is the consequence of a high dollar is balanced by higher
debt service costs and lower commodity prices for developing countries. Tomorrow a sharp and sustained drop in the value of the dollar
could produce — as it did in the seventies — major disruptive effects on international trade and finance. The policy question — unan-
swerable in the abstract — is whether a desirable one-time drop in
the dollar is conceivable. Or whether once the dollar starts weakening
it will be difficult to reestablish confidence. In economics as in other
fields the gods sometimes punish humanity by fulfilling its wishes too
completely.

Three *political* consequences seem to me to flow necessarily
from existing arrangements:

• One of the principal virtues of floating exchange rates — economic policy flexibility — too often has been turned into a vice. Countries have been able to support overvalued exchange rates by borrowing, or to encourage undervalued rates to foster exports. In practice, the system has allowed too much flexibility.

• Exchange-rate arrangements have been a profound source of political controversy among the industrial democracies for more than a decade. The political impact of unilateral economic decisions mortgages other relationships.

• Disagreement over exchange rates is the way underlying disagreements over broad economic policy goals and methods are made explicit. The exchange-rate regime now in place tends to magnify these differences but it does not cause them.

The fundamental issue is that the international financial system cannot be sustained indefinitely by unilateral American decisions, however advantageous these might be to us in the short run. Leaders concerned with cooperative international foreign and economic policies must undertake a systematic review in order to find the basis for new, more equitable, and less volatile exchange arrangements. Its test will be whether the industrial democracies are able to agree on coordinated economic policies. No international system can meet everybody's maximum demands; but it must respond to enough common aspirations so that maintaining the system seems more important to its members than insisting on any specific dissatisfaction. A system that does not meet this test — and the present system does not — is congenitally volatile.

THE POLITICS OF INTERNATIONAL DEBT

I have expressed myself on other occasions on the international debt problem — not always to the entire satisfaction of banking audiences. Let me begin by stating two propositions:

• In the seventies neither governments nor the IMF intervened seriously in the process for recycling the huge accumulated earnings

of the oil producers. The commercial banks thus played an indispensable role in cushioning the financial consequences of the sudden and
dramatic rise in oil prices. Had they not done so a financial crisis
would have occurred much earlier and under much worse circumstances. Nor did the banks go beyond conventional wisdom when they
geared their lending policies to the expectation of a continued rise in
oil prices and hence continued inflation.

• No doubt many developing countries grievously mismanaged
their economic policies. Without reform of the economic policies of
most debtors no amount of help from banks or governments can possibly be effective. But this reform requires a subtle and sensitive
judgment of what, especially in fledgling democracies, the traffic will
bear. The objective is or should be to encourage democratic, market-
oriented, responsible governments. We must not in the name of debt
settlement bring into power governments that challenge the whole
concept of free economies and free peoples. That is not a role in
which banks (even central banks) or international institutions are
either comfortable or secure.

Nevertheless, the governments of the industrial democracies
have stood aloof from a process which will determine the future of
North-South relations and the stability of the international system for
a long time to come. This ostrich-like policy has come to the end of its
possibilities. Debt management based on purely financial criteria and
negotiated by financial institutions involves the political survival of
too many governments in developing countries; the problem by
definition is not purely economic. In a conflict between banks and governments it is foolhardy to assume that governments will never follow
the populist demand to restrict foreign financial institutions or to declare some form of unilateral rescheduling. To rely on the existing
system of debt negotiation indefinitely is to play Russian roulette.

The conventional analysis — particularly in the United
States — holds that the worst is over, that the most heavily indebted
countries are on the way to recovery.

The past two years have indeed witnessed considerable
progress. The external deficit of several key debtor countries has
contracted markedly, at first through austerity produced by the re-

duction of imports; more recently through an expansion of exports. The increase in debt has slowed. Massive amounts of public and private debt have been rescheduled. Some corrective economic policies have been put in place, sharply reducing the hemorrhage of capital. There are even faint but hopeful signs of economic growth in countries like Mexico and Brazil.

Many of the bankers in this room would also add, I am sure, that no significant debtor has defaulted or unilaterally rescheduled on nonmarket terms.

All this represents an extraordinary achievement in crisis management. Jacques de Larosière and Paul Volcker have earned the gratitude of the international community for their courageous and farsighted handling of the emergency that has been thrust upon them by the reluctance of governments to touch the hot potato. The lending banks have cooperated with them to an extraordinary degree.

Still, I believe that the current system of debt management is reaching its inherent limit. The issue is not whether the financial terms which now seem to be emerging from commercial bank debt renegotiations are inappropriate. The banks have made a maximum effort to take into account the economic pressures on debtor countries. My concern is that the political dynamics of the process are now beyond what even the wisest and most farsighted financial institutions can reasonably be expected to handle by themselves.

The record of the last few years argues against the hopeful view that any one settlement will be final. In each round of seemingly unending negotiation creditors have felt obliged to yield a little more ground. Rescheduling agreements are reopened; terms negotiated in good faith yesterday are renegotiated today. Inevitably, they may be viewed as adjustable tomorrow as well. Such a process involves a high risk, at some point, of running out of control.

It is this uncertainty — coupled with worries about what future international economic and financial conditions might be — which in my view is at the heart of the apparent fragility of contemporary international financial markets.

The very flexibility of recent terms means that the banks have conceded almost the limit of what a profit-making institution can sustain. This would not matter had we reached the end of the process. I doubt seriously that we have, for two reasons. The history of the thirties suggests that the crisis in debt problems occurs not at the height of the crisis but when matters are improving. As the adjustment process begins to work, the political incentive to sustain it will weaken — even though in many cases the underlying economic imbalances will continue for a long time. Just as the United States and other major industrial democracies seem unable to divorce economic policy from short-run political concerns, developing countries — many of whom, especially in Latin America, are themselves moving toward democracy — could become caught in a dilemma that *bad* economics seem to make *good* politics, at least in the short run. And the banks have little leverage left once the repayment of principal has been stretched out into the indefinite future.

Future debt discussions will take place in an increasingly difficult political climate if the present framework is not changed. Many governments, most politicians, political parties, and the media in the debtor countries are adopting harshly nationalistic, anti-IMF, anti-bank rhetoric. One can try to console oneself that this rhetoric is for domestic consumption, that serious leaders know better, that unilateral rescheduling will make financial matters worse. This argument has undoubted merit. But in our world rhetoric tends to create its own reality. And if only one major country kicks over the traces it will be difficult for the rest to sustain the current course — unless the violator is made to pay a huge price which in turn could start a political crisis thwarting the objective of sustaining moderate, democratic, pro-market governments.

The adjustment programs demanded by the IMF are not technically unreasonable; what they lack is a political context beyond the power or responsibility of the IMF or banks and which these institutions have had to improvise because of the abdication of governments.

Sooner rather than later the terms of reference of the debt debate must be changed. The current ad hoc debt strategy led by private institutions and the IMF has given both creditors and debtors some much needed breathing space. The time should be used to change the framework of the dialogue. Debt service is after all not an end in it-self. It can even act against the long-term interests of the creditors if it results in the drain of capital from the poor to the rich. Viewed only from the narrow perspective of debt service, the creditors and debtors have somewhat conflicting objectives. On the other hand global growth — without which debt service is primarily an accounting ex-ercise — is a goal which farsighted leaders from both North and South should share. Such an approach should take account of two realities:

• Without improvement of the economic policies of the debtor countries no outside program of assistance, private or public, can have any long-term impact. Economic reform is needed in most debtor countries not for the sake of the banks or of the IMF but for their own welfare.

• The debtors should not be expected to extricate themselves from their difficulties by reform and austerity alone. The creditor countries must recognize that fundamental economic imbalances caused by forces outside the debtors' control contributed to the accu-mulation of excessive indebtedness. The explosion of oil prices in the seventies and of interest rates in the eighties turned a difficult situa-tion into a crisis. These imbalances can be resolved only by a strategy of global growth. A cooperative effort between the industrial democ-racies and the principal debtor countries on the political level is therefore essential.

The challenge is to recognize that the developing countries can-not grow without considerable access to foreign savings in a world which seems less and less prepared to invest in developing countries. Seen from this perspective, the economic and political elements of the strategy would change dramatically. Throughout the seventies the banks were asked to play a role — that of development financiers — for which they were not designed. But long-term development fi-nance, which is what most of the highly indebted countries need today, involves a major governmental responsibility — however un-popular such a view is in most industrial democracies, including our own. The economic cost of such a program would be minor compared to the consequences of a global financial and political crisis. If both creditors and debtors lift their sights, there is here the prospect of a compact that could put the relationship between the industrial democracies and the developing world on an entirely new basis.

CONCLUSION

We meet at a period of substantial American recovery. The economies of most other industrial democracies are improving as well, if more slowly. There seems to be at least some maneuvering room with respect to the debt problem. All this creates an opportunity to point the world economy toward greater coherence and brighter vistas.

One obstacle to this goal is the tendency of all democracies to make economic policy almost exclusively in a domestic context. Because of our vast economic power this is a particular problem for the US policymakers and their constituents. Most of the American public still view this country as being relatively unaffected by international economic developments. Our political process has not yet adjusted to the reality that the United States is steadily becoming *more* integrated into an international economy that is becoming *more* global. We must resolve the dilemma if we are to overcome chronic international economic instability. For our time and our opportunity require dramatic US leadership.

In 1944 the United States threw its influence behind building international institutions. A new and dynamic economic system gave impetus to an extraordinary global recovery. Today the need is the same and the stakes are even higher, for many more countries are now principal participants in international economic affairs.

The spirit that produced Bretton Woods reflected the realization that in the long run the national welfare can be safeguarded only in the framework of the general welfare.

All great achievements were a vision before they were a reality. There are many in this room better qualified to fill in the many blanks for an overall design. My major point is that the world needs new arrangements. A new burst of creativity is needed to eliminate our dangers and fulfill our promise.

INDEX

ABM (antiballistic missiles), 155, 173
Acheson, Dean, 10, 13, 16
Aden, 185
Afghanistan, 30, 42, 45, 115, 117, 147, 148, 180, 185
Africa, 30, 59, 68, 70, 71–75, 117, 148, 223
  See also specific countries
Agreement on the Prevention of Nuclear War (1974), 178
Andropov, Yuri, 113, 114, 117, 184, 186, 204
Angola, 45, 114, 147, 185
Arabian Gulf. *See* Persian Gulf
Arab-Israeli conflict, 51–55, 81–83, 93–109, 117, 118–119
Arafat, Yasir, 98, 99, 104
Argentina, 135
arms control, 32, 37–42, 65, 66, 153–163, 168, 183–184
  and balance of power, 37, 41
  and defense strategy, 37–42, 84, 172–179, 183–184, 185–186
  and NATO, 18, 37, 41–42, 123, 167, 203–204, 209, 210
  proposals for, 158–163
  and Soviet Union, 120, 161, 172, 176–179, 203, 204, 209
  and trade policies, 86, 120–121
  See also SALT; START
Arms Control and Disarmament Agency, 153
arms race, 113, 118–119, 154, 157, 160, 172
arms sales:
  to Cuba, 185
  to Central America, 185, 196
  to Middle East, 20, 94, 101, 118–119
Asia, 212
  See also specific countries

"assured destruction" strategy, 161
Atlantic Alliance. *See* NATO
Attlee, Clement, 11, 15, 21

B-29 bomber, 10
Baker, Howard, 39
balance of payments. *See* developing countries: debts of
balance of power:
  assessing, 63
  and China, 117, 142, 143, 145, 146, 147, 148, 149
  and East-West trade, 43, 44
  European, 4, 5, 8, 9, 13, 15, 60, 61, 80
  geopolitical, 41, 42, 45, 56, 64
  in Middle East, 56
  military, 21, 30, 31, 34, 37, 54, 55, 60, 61, 62, 63, 64, 65, 66, 80, 115, 116, 180, 182, 185, 211–212
  and NATO, 7, 211–212
  strategic, 17–18, 32, 34, 65, 66, 153–154, 161, 167, 168, 172
balance of terror, 154
Bank for International Settlements, 224
Barnes, Michael, 191
Begin, Menachem, 82, 96, 103
Beirut, 53, 81
Bentsen, Lloyd, 191
Berlin, 30
  airlift, 16
Bevin, Ernest, 9, 10, 15
bipartisanship, 186, 191, 216
Bismarck, Otto von, 56
Brazil, 127, 133, 222, 226, 228, 233
Bretton Woods conference, 88, 224, 228, 229, 236

Brezhnev, Leonid, 71, 113, 114, 117, 119, 142, 143, 204
Broomfield, William, 191
Brussels treaty, 16
Brzezinski, Zbigniew, 144
Bundy, McGeorge, 35, 169

Callaghan, James, 11
Cambodia, 115, 185
Camp David Agreement, 82, 97, 104, 106, 109
Canada, 118
Canning, George, 5
Carrington, Peter, 167, 209
Carter, Jimmy, and Carter Administration, 144, 180, 181
Catholic Conference of Latin American Bishops (1979), 192
Central America, 86
  democratization of, 192, 194, 196, 198
  economic development, 193–195, 198, 199
  economies, 192–193
  report of the National Bipartisan Commission on, 191–200
  US military assistance, 198
  USSR in, 185, 192, 196, 198, 199
  See also specific countries
"Central America Democracy, Peace, and Development Initiative Act" (1984), 195
Central American Development Organization (CADO), 194–195
Chamberlain, Neville, 12
Chatila massacre, 105–106
China, 117, 120, 222
  Shanghai Communiqué, 145
  and US, 141–149
  and USSR, 142–145, 146–148, 149
Churchill, Winston, 3–4, 6, 10–11, 12, 15, 17, 19, 21, 25
Clemenceau, Georges, 138
Coal and Steel Community, 13
cold war, 16
Colombia, 197
colonialism, 18–19, 69, 70, 222, 226

Common Market, 207
  See also EEC
communism, weaknesses of system, 24, 48, 67, 84, 116–119
  See also Soviet Union
Communist parties, 15, 24, 67–68, 114, 116, 117, 119
conservatives (US), 62, 116, 121, 122, 180
Contadora group, 196–197
containment, US policy of, 8, 16–17
conventional forces, 32, 34, 83–84, 120, 163
  of NATO, 30, 34, 35, 36, 41, 65–66, 169, 170–171, 172, 203–204, 208–210, 211–212, 213–214
  See also defense policy, US–West
Costa Rica, 193, 195, 199
"counterforce capability," 161
Crimean Conference (1945), 6
Crosland, Anthony, 11
cruise missiles, 173
Cuba:
  in Africa, 30, 45, 73, 107, 114
  in Central America, 185, 192, 196, 198, 199
  missile crisis (1962), 16, 30
currencies, international, valuation of, 131–132, 229
  See also exchange rates
Czechoslovakia, 12, 42, 181

decolonization, 68
default. See developing countries: debts
defense policy, US–West, 18, 33, 34–35, 36, 65–66, 83–84, 123, 155, 156, 208–210, 212, 214
  conventional, 30, 32, 35, 36, 41, 65–66, 83–84, 120, 163, 169, 170–171, 203–204, 208–210, 211–212, 213–214
  linked to arms control policies, 37–42, 84, 153, 154, 155, 156–157, 158–159, 163, 173–176, 183–184, 185
  single-warhead proposal, 158–163
  strategic, 32, 34, 35, 37, 65–66, 83–84, 120–121, 145–146, 153, 154, 155, 156–157,

158–159, 163, 168–172,
173–179, 206, 208–210,
211–214
and trade policies, 120–121,
148–149
See also conventional forces;
NATO; strategic forces
de Gaulle, Charles, 13
de Larosière, Jacques, 233
demobilization, after World War II,
10, 14, 30
democracies, industrial:
and East-West trade, 42, 43–44,
45–47, 86
economic policies, 128–129, 130,
131–132, 134, 137–138, 226,
231
and energy crisis, 133–136
policies toward developing countries, 20–22, 47, 72, 134–136,
232, 234, 235, 236
unemployment, 127–128, 130
unity of, 22, 23–24, 25, 29,
41–44, 46–47, 48, 68, 81, 85,
86–87, 88, 123, 187
and world economic crisis,
127–128, 130, 224
See also defense policy, US–West;
economy, world; NATO; Western
Europe
détente, 21, 84, 85, 114, 123, 143,
144, 146, 167, 180, 181, 183,
185, 206
deterrence, 31, 36, 214
developing countries (Third World),
47, 63, 128–129, 130,
132–133
debts of, 87, 127, 128, 132–136,
225, 226–227, 231–236
economic development, 60–61,
69, 72, 87–88, 132–134
emergence of, 68–72
and energy crisis, 133–136
and Marxism, 69, 71, 88
and USSR, 70–71, 72, 73, 75
Western attitudes and perspectives
toward, 3–4, 18–22, 69, 71, 72,
203, 204, 205, 215
See also democracies, industrial;
nonaligned movement; radicalism; Soviet Union: intervention

development finance, 235–236
disarmament, 30, 31, 85, 120, 161
Domenici, Pete, 191
Dulles, John Foster, 10, 21, 144,
154

East-West relations. *See* United
States: relations with Soviet
Union
East-West trade. *See* trade, East-West
Eastern Europe, 15, 44, 46–47
See also specific countries
economic development:
in Central America, 193–195, 198
and political stability, 7, 60–61, 69
of developing countries, 60–61,
69, 72, 87–88, 132–134
See also energy: crisis of 1970s
economic sanctions, 42, 43, 44–45,
85, 120–121, 148–149
economy, world:
crisis in, 127–129, 225
and debts of developing countries,
127, 128, 132–136, 226–227,
231–236
and the dollar, 131–132, 224, 230
effects of energy crisis, 127–128,
133–136, 231–232, 235
exchange rates, 131–132,
229–231
and nationalism, 222, 223–224
need for global perspective,
221–225, 236
in nineteenth century, 131,
221–222, 226
recovery and reform, 128–129,
130, 132, 137–138
and trade policies, 225–229
See also energy: crisis of 1970s;
IMF; trade *entries*
Eden, Anthony, 10, 12, 19, 20, 21
EEC (European Economic Community), 11, 13, 25, 134
Egypt:
and Israel, 53, 97, 103
and PLO, 52
role in Middle East negotiations,
53, 54, 55, 103, 106, 107
See also Camp David Agreement;
Suez Canal crisis
Eisenhower, Dwight, 19

El Salvador, 192, 196, 197, 198, 199

energy:
  alternative sources, 137
  coal-based, 226
  crisis of 1970s, 133–136, 222, 229, 231–232, 235
equilibrium, 4, 22, 23, 30, 62, 64, 66, 80, 115, 142, 146, 147, 179, 182, 221
  British role in maintaining, 5, 8, 12, 13
  nuclear, 17–18, 31, 65
Ethiopia, 45, 107, 114, 147, 185
Eureka proposal, 157–158, 159, 160
Europe:
  British position in, 5, 8, 11, 12–13, 15, 23, 61 80
  industrialization of, 222, 226
  See also balance of power; democracies, industrial; Eastern Europe; NATO; Western Europe
exchange rates, 130, 131–132, 224, 229–231

Facio, Gonzalo, 199, 200
Falkland crisis, 19, 21, 23, 86, 87
Federal Reserve Bank, 230
financial institutions, international, 224–225, 231
  and energy crisis, 132–136, 231–232
  and Latin America, 87
  need to restructure, 88, 132
  rescheduling debts of developing countries, 87, 134–136, 232–236
  See also economy, world; trade *entries*
first strike, 154, 155, 157, 162
"first use" renunciation. *See* no-first-use doctrine
Ford, Gerald, and Ford Administration, 105, 180
foreign policy, US:
  and Africa, 68, 70, 71–75
  and arms control, 37–38, 39, 66, 173–176, 183–184, 185–186
  and balance of power, 61–62, 63, 64, 80

bipartisanship and, 186, 191, 216
and Central America, 86, 191–192, 193, 194, 195, 196, 197–198
change and development of, 4–11, 16–22, 60–64, 79–81, 89
containment, 8, 16–17
and cooperation with industrial democracies, 47, 85, 88
toward developing countries, 18–21, 68–69, 70–71, 72, 88–89
and East-West trade, 42, 45–47, 85, 120–121
and energy, 137
in Falkland crisis, 19
and free trade, 137
future direction of, 79–81, 85–86, 88–89
and Latin America, 87–88
linkage in, 39, 42, 45, 46, 120–121, 174–177, 183–184, 185–186
in Middle East, 52–54, 55, 56, 81–83, 86, 93, 94–96, 97, 98, 101–110, 148, 206
in post–World War II era, 3–4, 6–8, 9–11, 13–18, 30–31, 60–64, 205, 207
and SALT, 122
in Suez, 19–20
after Vietnam, 8, 64, 168, 216
  See also United States
France, 19–20, 117, 128, 178
Franklin, Benjamin, 13

Gaitskell, Hugh, 12
GATT (General Agreement on Tariffs and Trade), 228
Gaza. *See* West Bank–Gaza
Germany, nineteenth-century, 9, 222, 226
  See also West Germany
Golan Heights, 108–109
gold standard, 129, 131, 221, 222, 225, 229
grain sales (US–USSR), 42, 44, 47, 85, 121, 223
Great Britain, 86, 178, 205–206, 222, 226

attitudes and policies after World War II, 3–4, 6, 9–10, 14–15
and developing countries, 18–19
economic policies, 128, 129, 135
enters EEC, 11, 13
Foreign Office, 3, 11
and Greek-Turkish aid program, 15
role in European politics, 5, 8, 11, 12–13, 15, 23, 61, 80
and Suez, 19–20
traditions of foreign policy, 3–5
and United States, 3–12
Greece, 128
Greek-Turkish aid program (1947), 15
Grenada, 205–206
Gross National Product (GNP), US percentage of, 8, 61, 79, 80
Group of 77, 69
Guatemala, 193

Haig, Alexander, 54
Harmel Report (1967), 37
Hitler, Adolf, 9, 61
Honduras, 192, 198
Hong Kong, 226
Hoover, Herbert, 7
Hopkins, Harry, 14
Howard, Michael, 3
Hussein, King, 55, 98, 103, 104

ICBMs (intercontinental ballistic missiles), 39, 40, 159, 160, 177
IMF (International Monetary Fund), 87, 135–136, 224–225, 226–227, 230, 231–232, 234, 235
India, 63, 100, 149, 222
India-Pakistan war of 1971, 19
Indonesia, 222
INF (Intermediate-range Nuclear Forces):
negotiations, 172–179, 183, 209–210
"walk-in-the-woods" formula, 176
inflation, 127, 131, 133, 223, 229, 232
Inouye, Daniel, 191
interest rates, 131, 133, 230, 235

intermediate-range missiles, 34, 173–179, 183
based in Europe, 203, 206, 209–210, 212, 214
international banking system. See financial institutions, international
International Trade Organization, 228
Iran, 10, 55–56, 69, 107, 110, 147
Iraq, 51, 56, 107, 110
Iskandar Ahmad, 108
Israel:
Arab-Israeli conflict, 51–55, 81–83, 93–109, 117
Camp David Agreement, 82, 97, 104, 106, 109
and Egypt, 53, 97, 103, 107
Golan Heights, 108–109
invasion of Lebanon, 51–53, 93–94, 97, 100, 106
relations with US, 95–96, 97, 98, 101–109
West Bank–Gaza, 52, 53–55, 56, 82, 93, 94, 95, 96–97, 98, 99, 102–103, 104–105, 107, 108, 109, 110
See also Palestinian question; PLO
Italy, 206, 222

Jackson, Henry, 191
Japan, 6, 118, 134, 138, 148, 222, 224, 228
Jerusalem, 54, 55, 95, 109
Johnson, Lyndon B., 155, 156
Jordan, role in Middle East negotiations, 55, 82, 86, 93, 94, 95, 97–98, 99, 103, 104–105, 106

Kant, Immanuel, 138
Kemp, Jack, 191
Kennan, George, 16, 35, 169
Keynes, John Maynard, 127
Khomeini, Ayatollah Ruhollah, 56, 110
Khrushchev, Nikita, 114, 117
Korea, 8, 16, 21, 30, 141, 148
See also South Korea
Korean airliner incident, 204
Kosygin, Alexei, 117

Latin America, 87–88, 133, 234
  See also specific countries
Lebanon, 117, 118
  Israeli invasion, 51–53, 93–94,
    97, 100, 106
  and the PLO, 52, 53, 55, 86
Lend-Lease program, 10
Lenin, Nikolai, 44, 115
Leninism, 115, 197, 198, 199
liberals (US), 62, 122, 180
Libya, 105, 115
linkage:
  defense policy and arms control,
    174–177, 183–184, 185
  and SALT, 39
  and trade policies, 42, 45, 46,
    120–121
  See also arms control; defense pol-
    icy, US–West
Llandudno (Churchill speech at), 17,
  25

Macmillan, Harold, 21
McNamara, Robert, 35, 169–170
Marshall Plan, 7, 8, 9, 13, 16, 61,
  138, 191
Marxism, 69, 71, 88, 142, 197, 198,
  199
Mathias, Charles, 191
MBFR negotiations, 209–210
Mexico, 87, 127, 133, 196, 222,
  228, 233
Middle East:
  Arab-Israeli conflict, 51–55,
    81–83, 93–109, 117, 118–119
  Camp David Agreement, 82, 97,
    104, 106, 109
  negotiations, 52, 54, 55, 82, 86,
    93–98, 99–100, 101–110
  Persian Gulf, 20, 52, 55–56,
    109–110, 137
  and USSR, 53, 55, 56, 82, 93–94,
    110, 117, 118–119
  West Bank–Gaza, 52, 53–55, 56,
    82, 93, 94, 95, 96–97, 98, 99,
    102–103, 104–105, 107, 108,
    109, 110
  See also Palestinian question; PLO;
    specific countries
Middle East War (1973), 118–119

military balance of power. *See* balance
  of power
military forces, conventional. *See* conventional forces
MIRVs (multiple independent reentry
  vehicles), 155, 156, 159, 160,
  161, 162
missiles, 39, 40, 142, 154–163 passim, 173–179 passim
  See also ABM; cruise missiles;
    ICBMs; intermediate-range mis-
    siles; MIRVs; MX missile; nu-
    clear submarines; Pershing II
    missiles; SS missiles; Trident sub-
    marine; warheads
Molotov, Vyacheslav Mikhailovich, 15
monetary policies, international:
  after energy crisis, 133–134
  need for reform, 132, 221–225
  of nineteenth century, 221–222,
    226
  See also developing countries;
    economy, world; exchange rates;
    financial institutions; trade *entries*
Monge, Luis Alberto, 195
Monnet, Jean, 13
Monroe Doctrine, 5
MX missile, 40, 161, 162

Nablus, 108
Nasser, Gamal Abdel, 20
nation-states, 70
National Bipartisan Commission on
  Central America, report of,
  191–200
National Endowment for Democracy,
  193
NATO (North Atlantic Treaty Organization):
  and arms control, 18, 37, 41–42,
    123, 167, 203–204, 209, 210
  conventional forces, 30, 34, 35,
    36, 41, 65–66, 169, 170–171,
    172, 203–204, 208–210,
    211–212, 213–214
  defense strategy, 18, 30, 33,
    34–35, 36, 37, 41–42, 65–66,
    84, 168–172, 208–212,
    213–215
  and developing countries, 25, 215

dual-track approach, 174, 175
and East-West relations, 180–187,
    215
evaluation of and proposals for,
    23, 25, 29, 37, 123, 167–168,
    187, 203–207, 213, 215–217
formation of, 7, 9, 16, 61, 205,
    216
INF negotiations, 172–179, 183
and North-South policy, 215
and nuclear weapons, 30–36, 84,
    168–179, 183–184, 206, 209
reorganization of, 208–210
restructuring role of Europe in,
    207–210
strategic defense, 30–31, 32,
    34–35, 41, 65–66, 83–84, 153,
    168–172, 173–179, 203, 206,
    208–214
strategy problems, 155–156, 159,
    160, 167, 168–172, 173–176,
    187, 203–204, 206, 207–208,
    210–211, 212–213
US position in, 8, 35, 203,
    204–207, 210, 214, 215–216
See also defense policy, US–West;
    democracies, industrial
neutron bomb, 177
New Deal, 8, 61, 128
New International Economic Order,
    132
Nicaragua, 193, 195–196, 198
    contras, 199
    Sandinista forces, 196, 198, 199
Nigeria, 133
Nitze, Paul, 176
Nixon, Richard, and Nixon Adminis-
    tration, 21, 142 155, 156, 180,
    181
no-first-use doctrine, 34–36, 84,
    168–172
nonaligned movement, 69–70, 72
    Group of 77, 69
    See also developing countries
North-South relations, 215, 232, 235
nuclear freeze proposals, 37, 38, 156
nuclear parity. See strategic parity
nuclear submarines, 158, 159, 162,
    177
nuclear war, 65, 66, 68, 154,
    156–157, 211, 214

doctrine of limited, 33, 34
public agitation over, 34, 35, 157,
    169, 170, 171, 172, 175
nuclear weapons, 21, 83–84, 120,
    142, 153–163 passim,
    168–172, 173–179, 182, 183,
    203, 206, 214
    NATO and, 30–34, 35, 168–179,
    183–184, 206, 209–215
    no-first-use proposal, 34–36, 84,
    168–172
    See also arms control; defense pol-
    icy, US–West; SALT; strategic
    forces
Nunn, Sam, 40

OAS (Organization of American
    States), 87, 198
OECD (Organization of Economic Co-
    operation and Development), 46
Ogarkov, N. V., 175
oil:
    current surplus, 137
    economic repercussions of energy
    crisis, 127–128, 133–137, 222,
    229, 231–232, 235
    See also energy
OPEC (Organization of Petroleum
    Exporting Countries), 132–136

Pahlavi, Mohammed Reza (Shah of
    Iran), 69, 223
Pakistan, 100
    India-Pakistan war of 1971, 19
Palestine, 10
Palestinian question, 51–53, 54, 55,
    94, 96, 99, 104, 105, 107,
    108
Panama, 197
Percy, Charles, 191
Peres, Shimon, 97
Pershing II missiles, 176, 177
Persian Gulf, 20, 52 55–56,
    109–110, 137
pipeline (Soviet natural gas) decision,
    42, 85, 86, 120
PLO (Palestine Liberation Organiza-
    tion), 51–53, 54 55, 82, 86, 94,
    95, 96, 98–99, 100, 104, 107
    See also Arab-Israeli conflict; Mid-
    dle East

Poland, 23, 30, 42, 45, 47, 48, 116, 117, 120
Potsdam Conference (1945), 6
protectionism, 130, 226, 227

radicalism, 43, 143
  in developing countries, 87, 88, 135, 206
  in Middle East, 51, 52, 53, 55, 56, 93, 98, 107, 108, 110
Reagan, Ronald, and Reagan Administration, 115, 180, 181, 183, 187
  on arms control, 37–38, 39, 40, 66, 153, 157, 176
  on China, 141, 144, 145
  Eureka proposal, 157–158, 159, 160
  and Middle East, 81, 82, 83, 86, 93, 94–96, 97–98, 99, 102, 104, 107, 108, 109
recession, 113, 127, 128, 129, 133, 134, 136, 137, 192
"Red Plan," 9
Regan, Donald, 132
revolutions, 20, 21, 55, 68, 72, 185, 196, 198
Rhodesia, 11
Ricardo, David, 226
Roosevelt, Franklin, 3, 6, 10–11, 15, 18, 19, 128
Rose, François de, 211

Sabra massacre, 105–106
Sadat, Anwar, 97, 99, 106, 107
SALT (Strategic Arms Limitation Talks), 38, 39, 41, 122
  approach, 156, 157, 160, 163
  I (1972), 155–156
  II, 39–41, 156, 157, 158, 159, 180, 181, 206
sanctions, economic, 42, 43, 44–45, 85, 120–121, 148–149
Sandinista forces, 196, 198, 199
Saudi Arabia, 55, 56, 106, 107–108
Schuman, Robert, 13
Scowcroft Commission, 161
Senate Foreign Relations Committee, 7, 191
Shiites, 55

Shultz, George, 98
  visit to China, 141–149 passim
Singapore, 118, 226
Smith, Adam, 129, 226
Smith, Gerard, 35, 169
Soames, Christopher, 25
socialism, 15, 70, 71, 128
Solidarity, 45, 120
South Africa, 59, 68, 72–75
South Korea, 118, 127, 222, 226
South Yemen, 45, 105, 107, 110, 115, 185
Southeast Asia, 45
Southern Africa, 11, 59, 75
Soviet Union:
  economic weaknesses, 24–25, 45, 48, 64, 67, 84, 88, 113, 118, 119, 182
  foreign policy, 117, 185–186, 187
  ideology, 115–117, 119
  intervention, 20, 23, 30, 41, 42, 45, 56, 65, 70, 71, 73, 107, 110, 114, 116, 117, 120, 185, 192, 196, 198, 199
  KGB, 116, 204
  in Middle East, 53, 55 56, 82, 93–94, 110, 117, 118–119
  military and weaponry developments, 23, 30, 32, 34, 37, 39, 40, 64–65, 94, 113, 115, 116–117, 118–119, 142, 153–154, 155–156, 158, 161, 169, 173, 175, 176–177, 178, 184, 211
  and NATO, 177–179, 183, 203, 204, 210–211
  non-Russian population, 24, 48, 67, 119
  policies toward developing countries, 70–71, 72, 73, 75
  political and bureaucratic stagnation, 24, 47, 48, 63, 64, 67, 84, 88, 114, 116–119, 121, 182, 186
  in post–World War II era, 6, 9, 15–16, 30, 142
  relations with other Communist countries, 117
  and SALT, 38, 39, 40–41

trade with West, 42–48, 85,
     120–121, 223
US–West future policies toward,
     21–25, 41, 45–47, 65, 66–67,
     68, 84–86, 88–89, 113–123,
     183–187, 215, 216
US–West past policies toward,
     14–18, 21, 37–38, 62,
     115–116, 121, 143–144,
     153–154, 180–181, 210–211
     See also balance of power; détente;
     United States: relations with So-
     viet Union
Spain, 117, 128
SS (surface-to-surface) missiles
     (USSR):
     SS-18, 40, 161, 162
     SS-20, 177, 178, 181
Stalin, Joseph, 15, 21, 32, 113, 114,
     117
START (Strategic Arms Reduction
     Talks), 41, 157, 159, 163, 178,
     179, 183–184
     Eureka proposal, 157–158, 159,
     160
State Department (US), 7, 11
strategic forces, 30–31, 32, 37–42,
     39, 40, 41, 65–66, 83–84, 153,
     154–155, 156, 157, 158–162,
     168–172, 173–179, 184, 211
     proposals for, 158–163
     and SALT, 38, 39, 41, 155–158
     See also defense policy, US–West;
     NATO; nuclear weapons
strategic parity, 33, 34, 161, 168,
     209
Suez Canal crisis, 10, 12, 19–20, 21
summit meetings, US–Soviet, 184
     economic, 25, 47, 138, 224
Sweden, 128
Syria, 51, 52, 53, 55, 108

Taiwan, 141, 144, 145, 148
tariffs, 129, 130, 225–226
technology:
     military, 18, 31, 32, 35, 65, 69,
     118, 119, 153, 154, 155, 156,
     158, 159, 168
     in nineteenth century, 221, 222

transfer of, 42, 44, 85, 120,
     145–146, 147, 148–149
terrorism, 115, 185
textile negotiations, 141, 145
Third World. See developing coun-
     tries
trade, East-West 23, 42–48, 85, 86,
     118, 120–121, 183, 223
     credit policies, 43, 44, 45–46, 47,
     85
     and debts of developing countries,
     44, 47
     linkage and, 42, 45, 46, 47,
     120–121
     and sanctions, 42, 43, 44–45, 85,
     120–121, 148–149
trade, international, 72, 131–132,
     136, 137–138, 225, 226–227
     free, 127, 129–131, 137, 222,
     225–228
     impact of dollar on, 230
     in nineteenth century, 221–222,
     226
     policy and politics, 225–229
     protectionism, 226, 227
     restrictions, 225, 226–227, 228
     US–China, 145–146, 148–149
Trident submarine, 162
Truman, Harry, 6, 14, 15, 21
Truman Doctrine, 16, 61
Turkey, 206

United Nations, 95, 109
United States:
     attitude during post–World War II
     period, 3–4, 6–7, 8–9, 13–14,
     16, 18–19, 25, 60–64
     and balance of power, 4, 6, 8, 60,
     61–62, 63, 64, 65, 66, 80
     and China, 141–149
     defense and weaponry, 18, 30–31,
     32, 39–40, 65–66, 83–84, 94,
     110, 113, 115, 120–121, 153,
     154, 155–156, 158, 161,
     168–172, 173–179, 183–184,
     185, 206, 209, 210, 212
     developing countries' view of, 70
     and draft, 36, 170
     economic and trade policies, 42,
     43, 44–45, 79, 87–88, 118,

United States (*Cont.*)
  128, 130, 131–132, 134,
    137–138, 148–149, 222–223,
    224–225, 227–229, 230, 236
  and Europe 13–14, 42, 81,
    83–87, 148, 167, 169, 172,
    173–176, 181–182, 186,
    203–207, 208, 210, 212–213
  grain sales, 42, 44, 47, 85, 121,
    223
  and Great Britain, 3–12
  and IMF, 224–225
  isolationism, history of, 4, 5, 8, 9,
    60, 206, 212
  loss of strategic superiority, 32,
    154
  military budget, 30, 36
  national security and strategic in-
    terests, 37, 61, 71, 86, 121,
    137, 146–147, 148, 170–171,
    192, 194, 195, 197, 200
  nuclear freeze proposals, 37, 38
  percentage of world GNP, 8, 61
    79, 80
  pipeline (Soviet natural gas) deci-
    sion, 42, 85, 86, 120
  relations with Britain and Europe,
    11–25
  relations with Soviet Union,
    14–18, 23–25, 30, 37–38, 41,
    42–43, 61, 62, 64–68, 70–71,
    84–85, 113–123, 142–145,
    146–148, 153–154, 172,
    174–179, 180–187, 204, 205,
    215
  trade deficit, 227
  in world economic system, 222,
    225, 227–229, 230, 231, 234
  See also defense policy, US–West;
    foreign policy, US; NATO;
    SALT; trade *entries*
US Congress, 7, 39–40, 120, 153,
    191, 195

Vance, Cyrus, 144
Venezuela, 133, 196–197
Versailles economic summit, 47
Vietnam war, effects on American

  policy, 8, 64, 118, 142–143,
    155, 156, 168, 180, 216
Volcker, Paul, 233
volunteer armies, 36

"walk-in-the-woods" formula, 176
warheads, 153–162 passim, 175,
    178, 184
Watergate, aftermath of, 155, 180
Weinberger, Caspar, 168
West Bank–Gaza, 52, 53–55, 56, 82,
    93, 94, 95, 96–97, 98, 99,
    102–103, 104–105, 107, 108,
    109, 110
  See also Palestinian question
West Germany, 6, 10, 117, 128,
    153, 204
Western Alliance. *See* NATO
Western Europe:
  defense of, 32, 33–34, 36, 83–84,
    120, 153, 173–179, 203–206,
    207–215
  and détente, 21
  and developing countries, 18–22
  economic and trade policies,
    42–48, 85, 118, 222–223, 224,
    226
  and PLO, 86, 98
  relations with Great Britain and
    US, 11–25
  role of, in NATO, 207–210
  traditional foreign policy, 8
  unification moves, 13–14, 23–25,
    207
  See also democracies, industrial;
    NATO
Williamsburg economic summit, 138
Wilson, Woodrow, 6
World War I, 6, 9, 131, 182, 226
World War II, 3, 6, 9, 14, 60, 141,
    153, 170, 182, 205, 216
Wright, James, 191

Yugoslavia, 149, 230

Zambia, 73
zero option, 175–176
Zimbabwe, 73